We need
a bigger boat

Some simple advice for changing your life
and saving your planet. *Eloram*

MICHELLE DUARTE

WildSpring
92978 Cemetery Loop, Box R
Port Orford, OR 97465
www.eloram.info

Publisher's Note: This is a work of fiction. Names, characters, places, and incidents are a product of the author's imagination. Locales and public names are sometimes used for atmospheric purposes. Any resemblance to actual people, living or dead, or to businesses, companies, events, institutions, or locales is completely coincidental.

We need a bigger boat/Michelle Duarte -- 1st ed.
ISBN 978-0692504024

Contents

Preface

Introduction

Chapter 1 – A new start   1

Chapter 2 – What on earth is happening with you   11

Chapter 3 – Life is not a goal, it is a path   25

Chapter 4 – Finding the great ocean within   39
Chapter 5 – Naked, in an empty room   53

Chapter 6 – Get out of your boxes   65

Chapter 7 – Opening your compassionate heart   81

Chapter 8 – What you believe, you live   93

Chapter 9 – Cleaning out the dark rooms, letting in the light   109

Chapter 10 – Feel what you feel   127

Chapter 11 – Karmic agreements and other children's stories   141

Chapter 12 – Knowing what to leave, knowing what to take   157

Chapter 13 – Relationships, that perfect reflection of you   177

Chapter 14 – What next   195

Afterward   207

Author   **212**

Acknowledgements

For Dean, who found me.

You shape the journey.
Eloram

The most beautiful thing we can experience is the mysterious.

It is the source of all true art and science.

Albert Einstein

Preface

THERE ARE TWO POINTS I'd like to make to help frame this unusual book:

First, this is not a book about conservation or eco-practices. It's not that those activities aren't valuable, but the real damage here is not because of what we do, it's because of who we are. This is a book about how we and the planet are linked on an intimate energy level, and to heal the planet, we need to start with ourselves.

Second, that over a quarter of the earth's population today believes in some form of reincarnation: about 300 million Buddhists, 800 million Hindus, at least 1 million of New Age religions. This is a foundational belief in this book. If you can't accept even the possibility of that intriguing process that allows you to balance your experiences and your choices, to try different lives and see what happens when you take different paths, you will have a very hard time embracing the rest of this.

Finally, this thought...Australian theologian, Neville Rowe, once said, 'We can believe we are on an evolutionary path toward God if we wish, or we can understand that we are already God experiencing itself.'

After the process of writing this book, I'm no longer sure there is a difference.

Introduction

IMAGINE A VISITOR from the stars who dropped by Earth some thousands of years ago. Who was so fascinated by it he decided to hang around and explore.

Imagine he could create a series of lives that he could inhabit, like an actor takes on a series of roles to play, in order to enjoy the life here and learn as much as possible about us.

And imagine he fell so much in love with our beautiful planet...and being human...he wanted to see what happens after we learn how to remake the world around us.

And to help if we screw it up.

At least, that's the hope.

{ 1 }

A new start

HELLO, I AM ELORAM.

'So what,' you're probably thinking. 'Who are you and what do you want from me?' is likely right behind.

Fair questions. But let's start with a few of my own: How tightly do you cling to your beliefs? How willing are you to let go of the familiar in favor of the alien? How open are you to ideas that seem without reason – literally, un-reasonable?

Maybe I need to ask instead, how happy are you? How well is your life working? Have all those familiar beliefs helped you create a life that brings you real satisfaction?

When is the last time you felt a deep and profound sense of joy, filled with wonder and gratitude at the rich panoply of life on this planet; so fascinated by the mystery of it all that life itself overflows your senses and you fall, almost swooning, in love with the possibilities.

When have you so loved what you were doing that the hours flew past as minutes, that you so looked forward to something with such fervor you were dizzy with anticipation.

And when, just when have you stood and stared into the face of the unknown, eager to jump into the darkness because that is where the secrets of your life are revealed. Where your future lives.

Perhaps, if you're very honest with yourself, if you learn to understand, master and control your – amazing – self, you can learn to create a life filled with satisfaction instead of resentment. Resentment that others have more than you...better than you. Resentment, the cancer of joy.

What if you could learn to open your mind - and your heart - to a reality that is far grander than you ever imagined. A reality in which there are no victims, no perpetrators, only choices, only lessons, only opportunities. A reality where, once you find the courage to take responsibility for everything that happens to you, for all you do and feel, you will learn how to create a life filled with joy....steeped in wonder....entwined with mystery and anticipation.... overflowing with pride at all you have done and seen and experienced and accomplished.

Now do you care why I am here? Have I offered enough carrot to continue? If your life contains all you desire, then it's unlikely you would even have noticed this book. But if you're at all interested in creating a better future, then why not continue with an open mind and heart.

So...who am I?

I'll get to that. First, how about what do I want from you?

There is a concept in your legal system that ties the credibility of the testimony to the credibility of the witness. The problem with that in daily life, however, is that a great deal of energy is then focused on the messenger, often at the expense of the message.

I ask not your belief at this point, nor even your acceptance. I ask your patience, that is all. The rest will follow.

So...I am a person, a consciousness who has chosen to live many different 'stories' in my existence...like an actor takes on roles in different plays. Each one chosen because it represents something I wished to experience, because it afforded me the opportunity to explore, first hand, some aspect of existence that suited my interests.

Consider that for a moment. It might help you better absorb what follows.

I was an explorer of possibilities, an adventurer who sought to experience the awesome diversity of life here. I came from the stars to your beautiful planet at the beginning of human time.

It was extraordinary. So filled with promise, with challenge, with unending beauty in all its incredibly rich expression that I chose to stay, for that was within my capability.

Please understand, when one fully realizes – within every aspect of their being – that they are part of the infinite God they can do such things. They can write their own stories.

Also understand that this realization comes not in the abstract, it cannot be held simply as knowledge. To know something is not necessarily to understand it; understanding comes from embracing it, by experiencing it. By experiencing all of it.

You might stop a moment to consider this as well.

I don't mean to continuously interrupt the unfolding of this grand story of your world and your role in this great drama; but in the purposeful contemplation of this text, you will find important truths and illusive insights that will seep off the two-dimensional page into your consciousness and form the foundation for the insights to come.

The benefits will be profound in your personal journey. On some level you must feel this, or you would not have been guided to this book. Consider yourself congratulated for paying attention.

Back to my story.

When I first came here, I did not wish to be but a visitor, as one who strolls through a playground and observes all the lovely children running around – so deeply involved in the thrill of their games and dramas they have forgotten the world outside the park.

I wanted to join them. I wanted to experience all they did, all they could.

I wanted to run until my breath turned to fire. I wanted to sing and feel the joy of my voice joining with others, to join hands and feel the touch of another's within mine. I wanted to roll on the grass and pick the flowers and smell the wind. To jump as high as I could and fall down and feel the press of other joyous bodies tumbling along with me. To build fires and swim oceans and climb mountains and conquer deserts.

I wanted to play, too.

So I chose to be as you on your wondrous world – a human being, with a mind and a body, with all your feelings and all your fears and anger and pain. And of course...your joy.

I wanted to experience it all. All. Life. Love. Rage. Grief. Birth. Death.

I have lived many stories here, many lives. I so immersed myself in this experience that it took awhile to remember who I was. A glorious reawakening, as you can imagine.

I will digress for another moment to reveal the answer to one of the greatest and most persistent questions among those of you who sense a greater existence beyond you: 'Why am I here; how could I possibly have chosen such a life, deaf, dumb and blind, bound by such painful limitation?'

In part, it is this: For that wondrous moment of 'Aha!,' of once again remembering that we are not an isolated island of consciousness, that we are not wretchedly alone, that we are instead truly a face of God, and for all time and all times an integral part of that transcendent state of unconditional love. It is in no small part for that intoxicating rebirth of infinity within us that we permit ourselves to lose ourselves in our stories.

Consider that, too, before you continue.

Once I remembered I was indeed God (and we do hope that the ego state in you does not recoil at the hubris you hear in that statement and remove yourself from the truth and insight behind it), I chose to come back once again as a human being, but with my memories intact, fully realized as a face of the infinite.

I then lived many lives as a teacher, planting seeds of awareness within gifted individuals, seeds that would begin to unfold when the time was right, when your evolution called for you to wake up and remember who you were, to remember your mastery.

If you are wondering why you found your way to this book at this time, look within. You will find one of those seeds, patiently waiting through millennia for the time when you were ready, when you had experienced enough, learned enough.

When you had bled enough and dreamed enough, had wept and wailed and learned through it all the blessings of compassion and the benediction of forgiveness. When you could pierce the veils of illusion and limitation and see that there is a much grander reality waiting in the wings for your awareness.

And, finally, you became ready to take those final steps to find your face of God within - that sacred, infinite part of you that knows how to be the creator of your own lives.

Welcome. It is good to feel your kind attention once again.

Now, I've come back this time not to live as you, but to make it easier for you to live as you, to help you wake up, and remember, and unfold.

For this is the time of new beginnings on your planet. I have come with many others to help in the birth of your new millennium. We speak in many different voices and in many different ways, and you no doubt find truth in some and disbelief in others. But the intention of all messages and messengers is the same: To make sure that everyone who is capable of seeing beyond the façade of this three-dimensional play will be ready for the next stage in your development. Some have referred to it in hopeful terms, like the ascension; others, less pleasant labels. People see the world not as it is, but as they are. No matter. Let's just call it the time of transition.

This is the time the prophecies have spoken of throughout your history. It is the time of choices, of ending one journey and starting another. It is the time when your world is coming to an end. If this makes you fearful, think instead what this signifies.

Know that to a caterpillar, when it looks into the future, all it can see is the cocoon. And, since it cannot conceive of the butterfly, all it sees is that truly its world will come to an end.

Also know that a prophecy is not a prediction, it is a warning. The ancient and not-so-ancient prophets were simply reading the probabilities that had been created by all the choices and experience that lead up to that point in their time. But you can change your agreements and shape the outcome of any event according to your wishes. All you have to do is learn how.

You are the caterpillars, and this is the time you have chosen as a species to emerge as those beauteous creatures whose wings flash their breathtaking colors as they unfurl in the sunlight. Or not. The choice is yours, the journey yours to make. Literally, to make.

When those around you cry, 'The world is coming to an end,' smile at them with all your love...and humor...and say, 'Yes, and isn't it wonderful. The world as we know it - with all its limitation and contention and violence and disease and corruption and sorrow - will end.'

This is why you have found me once again, to help you in this critical time on your planet, a time of great transition.

What kind of journey do you want to start when this one ends? How do you decide where to go next? And how do you actually start once you decide?

Like all great stories, it has to start with you. Each one of you has to make a choice, that when made together, create your future as a people. If you want to change your path, you have to change your direction. If you want to change your journey, you have to change how you move along it.

It's all about you. Who you are. What is important to you. What you want to take, leave behind, find. What helps you. What is in your way. You must refine what you see, where you put your attention and how you want each step to feel.

You. Seriously. That's what this is all about. You make choices and with those choices you create a life. Enough of you make the same choices and you create a future.

The turmoil you experience in your personal lives, you see in your world, you see projected throughout your society – great changes, great movements, great vast clashes of will in your reality.

All of this reflects the great clashes of will within yourselves. You look around the world and think why all of the indecision, the confusion, this unending difficulty. People fighting...they do not know what they want. Or they know exactly what they want and it's something that someone else has.

Your world is reflecting all of those parts within you that feel the same way about your life. You shake? Your earth shakes. You rage, and the weather obliges. You resent your neighbor and armies lay siege on one another.

And you look in wonder at the chaos in the world. Where do you think it comes from? More importantly, how do you fix it.

This is the end of one journey here. The time of transition to the next. You have little time to get ready for the curtain to come up on the next stage of your evolution. This is also why each of you has chosen to live on your planet at this time – when miracles become commonplace and the rules are changing, and you can even write your own rules. The time and space between action and reaction, cause and effect are shortening.

Look around you, you feel this.

Nothing applies that did. All is changing, because you are opening to a greater portion of the infinite. And I'm here to remind you, and to show you the path to once again find that part of you that is the God within.

To crumble the old, stifling belief structures that so shape your reality and limit your potential.

To process all the unresolved emotional burdens – from this life and others – that block your path and make your lives so painfully repetitive.

To enable you to transcend the myopia and boredom of your limited mind, and to once again connect with the infinite library of your unlimited mind.

To help you find your sovereignty. To help you find your mastery.

This is your new beginning as a planet. This is your new beginning as a species.

This can be your new beginning as a person – a fully realized creator of a profoundly joy-filled life.

It's your choice. All of it.

{ 2 }

What on earth is happening with you

LOOK OUTSIDE, LOOK AT YOUR LOVELY PLANET.

Many of you spend your time gazing at the stars, longing for someplace better, as though some enormous ship might come down and rescue you from your lives and carry you off to some great fantasyland. You wish 'If only I had a better life...if only I could do this, be that, be somewhere else.'

You can't imagine how many wait to come here for the pleasure of experiencing all that you do. It's that sweeping, immersive drama of your emotions that's the prize. The gifts of knowledge your emotions bring to you. The awareness. The experience. The wisdom. It is the interactivity with your emotions that turns knowledge into understanding.

Do you know what the purpose is in your being here? It is to feel. To experience. To be. It is to live. In your living, you find your mastery, and in this mastery you find your sacred self.

You are the masters, you created all of this – to learn much, to experience more. So that when you choose to pass into another reality – for the next round of your existence – you bring such gifts of understanding, of knowledge, that you add to the awareness of All That Is.

As I've said, you sign up for your lives like actors choose a role. You make lists of things you want to learn – which 'schools' you want to attend, which fascinating classes. Some of them might be dreadful, but you want to learn all that interests you, you want to become practiced and clever, you want to excel and attain great heights in your performance. You want to master this difficult and challenging reality in order to achieve your own mastery as an individual. You also want to balance experiences you had among your lives...a more complex discussion that we'll revisit later.

Some of this will feel impossibly hard. But if it was easy, it wouldn't be so satisfying when you get it right. If it was easy, you wouldn't have to become so strong in order to get it right. Think about this, too.

Not everyone can do this. Many don't choose the kind of demanding experience within this reality. It takes courage to come here and accept the rules of the game on this planet. The degree of difficulty is so high, the obstacles to full awareness so great, that your stories here can at times seem overwhelming, your lives unbearable. But, you can also attain extraordinary growth if you learn to master this unique environment, if you learn to overcome the handicaps you have accepted.

Think of all the riches you will have collected along the way in your journeys here, in your struggles and achievements. Think of the talents and strengths and skills you will have grown. Think of the immense joy of the oceans crossed, the mountains climbed. Think of all the gifts of awareness you bring back with you when you come 'home.' It is in your nature to find profound joy at adding to the wisdom of All through the depth and breadth of your experience.

You are fortunate to have chosen the kind of intensely full life that you find here, a life that you created. You are the creators, you just have forgotten that part of you. You don't think you know how, but you do. You will learn to remember, and this is the time that you've chosen to do so.

No matter where you are right now, look outside your window. See where you have brought yourself to in this life. Be still a moment and try to feel why you are here, and absorb the perfection of all you see.

This is your life. All of it. See that without all you have chosen, the sorrows and the happiness, your life would not shine. Without the hardship, you would not appreciate the joy.

Think about this, this is important for you to understand. Not simply as an abstraction, but as an authentic truth.

And consider this:

If you spend all of your lives on a flat, grassy plain...you're born, you live, and die on a flat, grassy plain...what would you learn?

You'd be lazy, you'd be weak, and you'd wind up rather stupid, don't you think.

But what if you wanted to make it more interesting. Let's say you build a mountain. Now, what does it take to climb your mountain? Remember, a mountain has vast cliffs, it has deep, dark chasms, overwhelming granite faces.

You realize you can't possibly make it by yourself, you must find others and you have to talk them into joining you. You must learn to work together. They have their own agendas, so you need to learn how to accommodate other people, how to respect another's sovereignty and timetable, how to learn from another's mastery. How to form a community and harness the power of many perspectives, gaining the benefit of many experiences.

You have to figure out the tools you will need to reach the top, and how to fashion them. To do that, you will need to develop a real understanding of the nature of your physical world. The properties of matter, the rules of its behavior, the sciences that will enable you to peer beneath the appearance of reality and explore its underlying truth. To see how to manipulate matter at your will, to combine it, shape it, fasten it, predict it, test it. And in all that exploration of the compounds and characteristics of your world, you cannot help but gain an understanding that your reality is not limited by what you see. Your reality is shaped by what you know.

So now, you have the team and the tools. Next, you must exercise, make your muscles strong and sure, expand your abilities and increase your skills. You have to learn what works and what doesn't. You have to train, to practice in order to build muscle strength and memory and to develop confidence in your abilities and how to handle things when they go wrong...and they will.

You learn to explore your world with the impetus of your goals and to master your environment with the focus of your will.

Nice payoff, is it not.

When you come here to your planet, you make choices that shape your life, that determine what you wish to spend your time doing, where you wish to focus your attention. What do you think will be more satisfying? Climbing great mountains, or sitting on a plain contemplating your navel.

This is what life is. You find the mountains you have chosen, and then you climb them. And then you find a stream and you jump in. Then you find fire, and discover what it can do. And you learn how to take the stream, and the mountain, and the fire, and create a life.

You burn yourself, and all but drown when you don't know how to ford the stream. Sometimes you don't prepare properly and you fall off a cliff. So you have to try again. You learn endurance and trust and confidence. And at the end of your life, look at all you have accomplished, all you have learned to do, simply because you chose to make it interesting.

You have all chosen lives to make it interesting for you. Celebrate this. Revel in it. Do not look at the heavens and rail against a God who imposed this hardship on you, for you are the one that chose it and you are the one who will reap all the riches of it.

Allow yourselves to look at all you've known and celebrate your strength, your courage, and your mastery. You have each one of you chosen great challenges and difficulties. There have been times you feel you've made an overwhelming error: 'I could not have chosen this.' You did. Acknowledge it, own it, and in that owning, you assume the power within it.

Are you resistant to this? Do you find it easier to blame others for the misfortune that finds you?

If you believe you didn't choose this, do you know what you are admitting? That you are a victim, that you have no power, you have no control over your life, that you are subject to another's will.

You have just given over all your sovereignty to someone else. Don't 'yes, but...' yourself into being a child.

Own your lives. Own the difficulty, the hardship, and feel pride in all that you've done, all that you've learned, all you've accomplished, all you have survived and mastered. You have such abilities. Recognize them. Enjoy them. Exalt in them.

When something hurts, thank it for the lesson it gives you. When something makes you angry, thank it for the information it reveals. This is what life is about – the richness of experiencing the lives you have created and the satisfaction of accomplishing great feats in the face of seemingly insurmountable difficulties.

Now, let us talk about the difficulties that you are all experiencing in this time in your reality. Things have been shaken up quite a bit of late, haven't they. Earthquakes. Tsunamis. War. Disease. Extinctions. Even the climate has seemingly turned on you.

You are all experiencing and observing earth changes that will manifest throughout your planet's transition.

Does this confuse you? You feel you are one entity, your planet something else entirely.

There is no difference between you and the rest of the universe. You and your planet are inextricably entwined, you are made of the same frequencies of energy that have translated themselves into the same matrixes of matter; you share the same fields, you inhabit the same time and space. You feel your planet, your planet feels you. You share this with all living beings here, you simply have overlaid the sense that allows you to feel that energetic entente. You have layered over this connection with your rational mind that measures your reality, and by measurement, establishes boundaries that acknowledge separation where in truth there is none.

The simpler forms on your planet know their survival depends on reading that connection. If a great earthquake is coming, the birds know and take off to the safety of the sky. The dogs know and howl to warn their masters.

Many of you who have been able to access that part of yourself that feels this tie with your planet, you feel a pressure in advance of the vibration a great event brings, though not necessarily on a conscious level. It's like a 'bow wave' when a boat pushes a wave in front of it. Many of you know something is coming, and those who chose not to participate in this drama, they move to a place unaffected by the event.

Understand that when there is an event of great scope, it's because of the agreement of everyone in that area. Also understand that the event has meaning within the larger reality of your world, as well as within your own individual lives.

There are those who choose to observe it. Ask what is the lesson of looking at such an event, at seeing the destruction, the terror, the loss, the pain and death. Empathy. Understanding. To open up the compassionate heart. For some, it is an opportunity to break down the barriers between groups, between individuals. A shared trauma binds people together, a helping hand crosses boundaries of prejudice and separation.

Do you understand what compassion means, what empathy means? You have found a way to let go of the illusion of separation between you and another. You see that they share the same emotions, the same hopes and fears as you. You see there is no difference between you and them. You see there is no such thing as 'them.' It is all 'we.' You see a glimpse of the greater truth, that you are all simply different faces of God.

Sometimes it takes great events to remind you of this, so that you can open your compassionate heart and accept someone else and feel what they feel. Such events are great lessons in your reality.

For those who choose to participate in it – for indeed it is a matter of choice – perhaps they choose to learn how to help their neighbor in need, or to heal the great wounds that had been caused by earlier traumas in that area, traumas that created schisms for example, between races and strata of society.

In many massive events, those who wished to lose, say, an addiction to physical goods, lost greatly.

And if someone who grieved because they had lost some precious trinkets looked at another who's entire home was crushed. Would they not feel how lucky they were? They learned proportion, they learned context, they learned to look beyond their self-absorption to see another's perspective. And in that, they learned to transcend the separation between individuals.

There are also those who choose to leave this world through these events, and that, too, is their choice. For when you come here, you have many choices regarding how you wish to leave your life. Sometimes you make your choices based on a simple desire to try something new, or to learn something through the experience itself.

Sometimes, you wish to create a death that could serve as a lesson for others. There is little that arouses the compassionate heart in your world more than the death of a child. In a great earthquake in your city of the angels some years back, a young girl chose to leave this life when her house fell down that hill; she gave a grand service in your world and is in great joy for it. The world grieved for her and her family, and in that grieving, felt pity for another. And in that, transcended their own illusions of self-absorbed isolation.

There are as many lessons to be learned from participating in such an event as there are individuals who participate. Great events teach great lessons. Everyone has something to learn.

There have been many such events around your world in recent decades, and there will be more. Wars. Raging weather. Vast cruelty against people of other religions, other races, other ethnic origins, against women and children. Some of these events will become tremendous lessons to help people reprioritize their lives, their thinking, to open their hearts and minds and release old prejudices, old angers.

It is important for you to understand that the lessons you face have been called for by your need to create events to help you grasp certain truths. What happens in your reality is nothing more, and certainly nothing less, than a reflection of the changes occurring within all of you.

Are you not all feeling shaken up in your lives. Have you not all undergone and are undergoing earthquakes within your lives. Whatever you held onto so tightly – like children holding a last scrap of its security blanket – you are being forced to pry your fingers open and let that fabric go. This is what you are all going through in your lives, your work, your relationships, your very beliefs.

You who are truly so tied to your earth, can your earth not reflect what's going on within you. This will only continue. You are all in this time going through great changes as the earth assumes a higher vibration, and as you work to assume a higher state along with her.

All are being challenged to make their leap, to find a higher mountain to climb.

But also understand this. Not all wish to let go of that scrap of blanket. Not all wish to leave that grassy plain or leave behind the pretty things they've collected all their lives, the things they believe prop them up like crutches, propping up someone who has never developed the muscles to stand on their own two feet.

So they set up great barriers, great obstacles that get in the way of their evolution, their mastery. 'I cannot do this,' they say, 'I cannot live without this, I refuse to change my thinking. I'm not going to consider a different reality.' And so they sit there like great slugs. Unmoving. Unyielding. Static. Giving nothing, gaining nothing, growing nothing.

But imagine that they are surrounded by people who are trying very hard to move, to grow. And imagine all these tiny points of dark energy that are stuck unmoving, surrounded by light energy that is working very hard to increase its brilliance, its vibration. There are great disparities of intentions as they conflict with each other, and in this, a great pressure builds. Finally, like the plates of your earth, they strain and push and pull and begin to move. They shake and plunge and slide against each other. In the end, when the dust settles, they assume a different relationship with each other.

This is what is happening around your world.

There are areas that call for great clearing and so you have fires that sweep your community. You have a need to wash yourselves clear of your old selves and beliefs and feelings, so you have great floods – a five-hundred-year flood in the middle of your country, the most difficult winter in your Europe's memory. Look to the weather around your planet to break your records as it reflects your own need to exceed old boundaries, and as the pressure increases between those who wish to evolve and those who don't.

Isn't it interesting…that it is now, along with all these other great physical events, you see changes sweeping your society as well. Think of the changes of the beliefs in your world, beliefs that shaped a reality you thought would always be there. Old political structures, crumbled. Even the Berlin Wall fallen, apartheid dissolved. Systems that enslaved gone. Yet new hatreds emerging. New reasons to subjugate others created. There are those who bitterly rail against any changes, and they set up a backlash that threatens the changes in the first place. And so you have huge waves of events that push back and forth over an issue in order to ensure that everyone on your planet sees it and is forced to see the results of such a conflict…and is forced to create common ground among the participants.

Of course the energy disparities are great. Of course they will manifest as great changes. This will continue in your reality.

The more energy that is put into resisting the changes, rubbing up against all of the energy that you are putting out to make those changes, this will create great and greater events around your world.

There will be more whose courage has chosen to participate, to observe, to leave. Think on these people as you see their stories in your news. Think why they would do such a thing, why they would choose to create such cataclysmic events in their communities, in their individual lives. Send prayers of healing to those that are being so shaken, so traumatized around your world.

Now, understand something else, something even more important:

The earthquake we referenced in your city of the angels...understand that the 6.8 earthquake was originally to have been a far greater event - an 8 in your measurement. Again...recall some of the prophecies about that area.

But there had been so many advanced souls called back to the city, masters of energy, who left and returned, who had wanted to leave and could not, who were activated and accelerated in their abilities...that they anchored the energies within this area and ameliorated the tremors greatly.

Masters of energy? Those who understand how to use energy for the highest good of those around them – though that understanding might not be on a conscious level, nor does it have to be. Your soul, your face of God, is the one who knows how to access and manipulate the energies for this reality. It does not take conscious intent by your personality, your ego, in order to do so. It only takes a clear connection between your soul and your personality, though we will speak more of that later.

The truth is that you are all capable of being such masters, and you each have the seeds of enlightenment within you, waiting for activation. You will each learn to use your loving and generous energies to help your planet and all those on it during this time of transition to help smooth out the conflicting energies that can create such hardship, such violence, such destruction throughout your world.

Know that in your city of the angels, you created enough connection with light energies that you pushed the darkness away. You created an event that simply hurt, but did not destroy. Celebrate this. It is a great accomplishment.

Understand that what you did for this area is also a reflection of what you have done for yourselves. Allow yourself to feel stronger and in more control of your destiny; feel that you are the creators, that you are no one's victim. You helped stop an earthquake that would have flattened a city.

This is the time to find your mastery, to connect with your face of God – your Godself – within; to explore it, embrace it. To find those parts of you that are not in harmony, and to find a way to bring greatest light into those parts.

So you can bring more light to your beautiful planet.

{ 3 }

Life is not a goal, it is a path

THIS IS A TIME OF GREAT TRANSITION FOR YOU, many of you spend your time gazing at the stars, longing for your lives, for your world. You reflect and shape that which goes on in your physical reality.

You are all like the earth. You have great plates within you of structures you have built up all of your lives – structures of beliefs, of emotional states, prejudices, pictures, expectations created by all your hopes and dreams.

Few, however, are your own; so many of them imposed upon you by the society in which you find yourself. Created by your parents, by their parents. By your friends and their friends. By your books and your movies and your leaders and your media. By your history as a people and your experiences as a person. By the rules and inertia of your third-dimensional existence.

Ever more so lately with the explosion of what you call social media that acts like a great blanket smothering everything with instant homogenization and fatal judgment. Fatal because of its immense power to limit your own ability to observe and assess. It maims your ability to discriminate good ideas from the merely popular. It kills your senses and codifies factions.

But this is the time you – and your planet – have chosen to battle and hopefully cast off outmoded and constricting structures, and overcome even the new siren song of mindless social connectivity.

As your earth is undergoing its change – and you are all reflecting this and driving it as well - there are parts of you that are ascending, evolving faster than others, as is happening throughout your world. And so those different parts...structures...rub up against each other, creating friction, creating pain.

But after that terrible earthquake, mountains next to your city of the angels were pushed three feet higher than before. A metaphor, don't you think.

Use the pain to see where the old and the new, the outmoded and the evolved are in conflict. To see where you need to put your attention and your energies to find a more serving path to a more satisfying future.

This is the time for you to achieve that elevated state, but the events continue to crowd in on you, one after another after another, taking away your energy, your focus, your will.

It only hurts as long as you insist on holding onto things that are not for your highest good – like a child holds onto a beloved tricycle. Children are afraid of the unknown because they can't control what they don't already know, and the risk of only two wheels may feel too great.

It's hard to let go of those things that are comfortable, but it is very important to make room for greater experiences in your life.

Understand that as a society and as individuals, you are growing as a child grows, and those things that gave you pleasure earlier in your evolution are becoming boring and are limiting your development.

You have all known boredom in your lives. Certain things that gave you great pleasure, no longer do so. This is a wonderful sign in your progress. Boredom is an indication you have learned all there is to learn within a particular experience. That which bores you is telling you it's time to move on.

If you insist on clinging only to what is safe, the part of you that is God – that part that ordered your life and chose the lessons ahead and chose all that you intend to accomplish – is moving you along to all those lessons that you originally signed up for. And if you don't want to leave the familiar and go on to the next class, you cling like children onto your old beliefs, your old security blankets. Then you find that it hurts terribly when these things must be taken from you. If you don't give them up easily, you may be forcing them to be ripped from you for your highest good.

Think of your future as a garden. What flowers do you want to grow, what foodstuffs do you want to plant. It's pleasant to spend your time daydreaming of whatever beautiful garden you desire, but it takes effort to make it real. What does it take to make your garden ready - is the land fertile, is it covered with weeds, rocks, what must you do to clear it, prepare it?

Let's say there is a vast overgrowth of brush that chokes out all productive future life. You know what they do in such areas on your planet...they set it afire to clear the ground.

You are the fertile ground of your own future and this is the process that you are all choosing to go through now.

It's not pleasant to be raked, to be picked clean, to have much that was familiar and dear to you burned away. The roots of those things ripped from your lives carry your blood and leave wounds behind. Wounds which only add to your pain, wounds which must be healed to move on. A self-limiting, increasingly painful cycle.

The only thing you can do is to trust that the universe is not a place that wantonly does such hurtful things to you. The universe simply provides whatever you have ordered, over and over again, like a great cosmic copier. For you are your creator, and you are the ones who know what you need – for whatever reason you have determined.

Those of us who are part of the 'manifesting' mechanism of the universe are like the waiters who bring what you order. Or, perhaps we are more like loving teachers...if your personality, your ego asks for nothing but daisies and ice cream, we will instead work with your soul to help you see how to ask for something more appropriate for your highest good.

What you've all been creating in your lives lately has been painful. What you've experienced has been a series of events that has forced you to look at parts of yourself that you've been very, very good at hiding from.

In each one of you, you have been forced to hold up a mirror. Sometimes the mirror was dark, sometimes distorted, sometimes it had barbed wire on it, trying to keep you from seeing what you did not wish to look at. But you created the mirrors yourselves, to enable you to see those parts of yourself that you needed to understand, that you needed to heal.

There have been earthquakes in each one of you. Fires, floods, hurricanes. There have been deaths. You have been creating events in your life that represent those parts of yourself that need your attention. Everything in your life has all been reflecting that which you require within.

Think of those parts of yourself that have held you from joy. Those parts that held anger, pain, that behaved as a wanton, spiteful, sulking, destructive child when confronted by bitter disappointment. Don't think that the unhappy little childself within you needs to die for you to find your maturity. It needs to be loved. Envision integrating that sad, angry part of yourself that has been outside of the energies of the light.

Bring it into your spirit and embrace it. Embrace the prodigal son, the one you could not control; embrace it within your being. Take the riches of all parts of yourself, even the ones that you call inadequate, that you consider unworthy and have labeled incorrigible. Take them within, ask them what they need to tell you. They have valuable messages about your identity, about your abilities, about your history and your pain that will tell you what you need to overcome in order to find your wholeness and your joy. They have strength and they have courage to have faced what they faced, and they will help you become whole.

It is only when you put parts of yourself outside - because you judge them as lesser – that you continue to be fragmented and unable to bring your life into harmony.

You continue to create events that reflect that unwanted fragment, one after another after another, so that you will finally open that door within yourself and find that part of you that you have put in the corner because you judged it an awful child. Your soul does not want any part of your being to be shut away. It wants you to notice that sad, neglected part and find a way to blend it within your entire being so that you will become whole.

So, your soul creates events that bring the child in front of you, who then creates intense emotional reactions to that event – rational or not. Do not label these emotions as good or bad. They simply are. Emotions are the messengers from you to tell you about yourself.

Your emotions are 'e'-mail, giving you instant insights into the parts of yourself that you have hidden away behind all the doors and mazes within yourself.

You are all quite clever. Your unlimited mind is infinite in its power and perspective; it holds the window between the you in this life and the All that ever has been, is, and shall ever be. But your limited mind – the narrow parts of your awareness that you have activated up to this moment – is just those parts that have observed and stored the experiences and the information you have been exposed to in the few years you have walked on this planet in this life.

But how many millennia have you each lived over and over again, here and elsewhere.

Imagine how much richer your existence would be if your limited mind could access your unlimited mind, could find the doorway to all you have ever lived, all you have ever known, to the great library of the infinite universe.

How to get the connection between that limited mind to that which can be called the super-consciousness, the unlimited mind...the Godself?

You achieve it through awareness, through becoming integrated with your soul. You find those parts of yourself that you have judged, and in the judgment imposed limitation and separated yourself from them, those parts that you have put behind bars and said, 'This is not acceptable.' Then you look on those parts within yourself without the compartmentalization of labels.

There is no good. There is no bad. There simply is. That is all.

There is no judgment, not outside of yourself. We don't judge you. God surely does not. God is not some vengeful old man who follows you around with a report card. You are the only ones who do that to yourselves.

Take a good look at yourself, take every part of yourself that has ever been, every thought, every feeling, every experience. Take those things that are deep and dark and hidden, that you barely even admit to yourself. Take every terrible wish you have ever felt for another who has harmed you, take every spike of anger, every resentment, every jealousy, every rage. Take everything you have labeled dark, evil, stupid, put it in front of you and love it.

Love it.

Think what these parts of your being have brought to you in awareness. They have helped you explore all that you are, to expand and shape your soul. It takes courage to have done such things and to do such a thing. Own who you are, let go of the labels. All within your being is a wealth of wisdom, waiting to be realized.

Think of yourself as a great library. There is not a good book nor a bad book. Each book simply explores an aspect of life, your life. It adds to the knowledge of the whole, it enhances your soul.

Once you can accept yourself as a unique part of the infinite universe - without judgments or separation, no good, no bad – then your lives will no longer behave like your planet's crust. You won't have parts of yourself rubbing up against other parts, pushing furiously against those areas that do not wish to move. You will not need to be so brutally shaken up in order to capture your attention... so you will finally face those parts that you have put behind a dungeon door.

Look at what those different parts feel. Where you feel discomfort indicates where you are resisting change. That is where the pressure will increase. Where you feel cracks beginning to form, that is the point of growth...the point where you can learn more about yourself and expand your beingness.

It is the point where your own mountain can become three feet higher. Do you begin to understand?

It doesn't have to hurt. It only hurts while you hold on to the old selves out of fear. Lose the fear. You won't fall...the earth at those cracks, those points of stress in your being, will not open up and swallow you whole. Send love where you feel the most stress, send acceptance where you feel the greatest pressure. Love those schisms within yourself into wholeness.

Love is the frequency, the universal frequency of healing, of unconditional acceptance. It contains no judgment, no qualifications, no conditions. And in that absolute allowing of all that exists is a chance to heal yourself into wholeness, to become all you are capable of.

There are vast numbers of people who have become quite adept at creating this loving frequency, this grace, within your reality. Much work is being done by these evolved individuals, much energy is being created to smooth out the cracks throughout your world. This is being reflected in your reality, which is slowly becoming richer and lighter. See this in the changes taking place everywhere. Your planet is showing signs of enlightenment in between the angst.

But there are parts that are more resistant than ever before; those still bound by their fears are becoming louder and more strident. They create great disturbances in certain locations around your world, and will continue to do so with increasing frequency and intensity. There will be some areas of your planet that will reflect these schisms of beliefs in terrible manifestations. You have seen shadows of some of these in recent years.

There will be great sadness in these events, but these have all been agreed upon by all those who participate. You must trust in this, and trust that in each event there is a purpose for everyone who chose to play a part in that drama; and there is much wisdom to be gained by the knowledge and experience from within such events.

When you see people ennobled by the compassion, the charity formed in their hearts by wrenching tragedy, or strengthened by the bone-crushing challenges in front of them, forced to reevaluate old beliefs, old patterns, old behaviors, trust it is for a higher purpose.

Know that everything you see in your world has a great lesson attached, and in that lesson, there is profound opportunity for enlightenment for everyone involved. That is why even those you would label victim, or those you would judge perpetrator, they have all volunteered. Some of them sacrificed parts of themselves for the greater good. They wanted to experience what that event offered, they wanted to master the wisdom embedded in the lesson.

There are no accidents. It is all by agreement. We do not exist within a random, chaotic universe.

We are all here because of one thing: Love. Love is what has created all of this.

Love is not the desire to possess, to judge, to control, to manipulate or direct. It is not a salve nor a grail. It is not romantic attachments nor familial regard. As we've said, love is unconditional acceptance.

Think of parents who love their child no matter what. No. Matter. What. They likely do not approve of everything the child does, but that doesn't effect their love. They understand sometimes their child must put its hand on a hot stove to learn what serves and what doesn't. So they accept even without approval their child's choices, trusting that is what the child needs to learn and how they have chosen to grow. Do you imagine God is less than those loving parents?

Love is unconditional acceptance, the absolute allowing of all that is, allowing each individual the respect of their sovereign choices...knowing that all choices eventually lead to a greater awareness of all that is. We keep telling you this because it is the most important thing for you to hear.

Can you not learn to love yourselves in this way? There is great richness in your lives and in all of you. We who have come here to help do not judge you, we love you greatly. How can we not. You are the ones who have created your world and you are the ones who are saving it. Life is not a trial nor a test, life is meant to be a joy; and the sadness you experience is just because you do not understand that you are loved and not judged, and there is nothing you do that will not eventually lead you to your Godself...no matter how long nor circuitous a route you take.

Do not let others put labels on you, no matter what their titles are. You are the masters, be careful whom you follow. Do this: Look in a mirror. That is the only one you should follow, that is the one who is your leader, the one who carries what is true for you from your Godself.

When you listen to those around you, imagine that you are holding this mirror up. What does the mirror say? Listen to yourself, learn to hear the voice within you, the moral compass within your soul that guides you to your personal truth. Ask the universe for help and it will be given to you, but you must be the one who hears it, you must be the one who feels the rightfulness of what is sent to you. Listen to others for information and guidance, but do not follow blindly anyone outside of your mirror.

In this learning to trust who you are, to love yourself unconditionally, you will find your mastery.

You see, by the act of learning to trust yourself, you are reprogramming your being. You are each a process...you are not a 'thing,' your lives are not a series of events. You are each a path. And what you attract to you brings you the knowledge to make your lives go where you wish. You are not an object, you are the process of becoming. You are the process of becoming the God that is each one of you, that sacred self which is your legacy.

Do not hold up in front of you this great vision, 'If I become this - richer, smarter, thinner - I will be perfect.' These are not worthy goals. You are not a point in some future time where all will be wonderful because you have finally attained your vision of self...but only after certain events and situations have taken place. You are the path that moves you closer and closer to union with your soul, where you find your Godself, the sacred face of the infinite God.

What you do on the way is the experience you have chosen to facilitate your journey, to make it interesting, entertaining, worthy of your goals, worthy of your soul. Why shouldn't you enjoy it.

And don't think of your path as a series of points on your way to your real life. You are your life. You are your choices, your desires, your priorities. You are the steps, you are the road. Everything, even your hand on the hot stove, adds to the fullest expression of your soul.

Look at everything in your lives as something that has been brought to you, at your request, to help you become the grandest, most wonderful being without limitation.

There are parts of you that are sore from having your great plates of belief and disbelief, of acceptance and denial, of trust and fear strain against each other all this time. That hurt from being bruised and burned. We can help heal that. There are many in your reality who have come to help you, and we all do it for love. We do it because we think not that you are in need of being 'fixed,' we do it because you are perfect in our eyes and we revel in every new state of perfection that you achieve.

Because we love you.

{ 4 }

Finding the great ocean within

YOUR REALITY IS FILLED WITH EXPERIENCE that expands and refines your being, designed to work with your different senses to impact your own energetics.

Like music...harmonics of vibrating energy that one of your physical senses absorbs in order to affect your emotional state. The kind of music you like says much about who you are, at least at that moment, and what kind of stimulation is appropriate for you, also at that moment.

There is very aggressive music, where the energetic impact on your being is quite intense. There's music that pats you all over, that soothes and calms you, like effervescent bubbles in a warm bath. There's music in which there are few harmonics, in which you impose your own structure onto the sounds.

Music is a fine invention of this reality, one of many. It enriches your incarnate experience greatly, allowing you to express emotions that you might not have the words to do so otherwise. It also serves to stimulate various parts of your physical, emotional and mental bodies and is a wonderful barometer, showing where you're in need of attention.

Music with a strong beat – sometimes judged appealing to your 'baser' nature...as though any part of nature could be base... operates at a lower frequency or vibration within the total harmonics of energy that comprise your unique self. To listen to it will stimulate the energy centers located in the lower areas of your body (some cultures call these focal points 'chakras,' located roughly along the path of your spinal chord).

To desire such stimulation could mean that you need a stronger connection to the energetics of your planet, that you need to more fully open your lower energy centers – sometimes called your survival chakras. Or, it could mean that you are only comfortable in those frequencies and need stimulation in others. If you look within, you will see the difference.

Music that has no beat, that winds its way like a bird through the sky, many instruments entwining and flowing together, tends to have a wider range of frequencies or vibrations. It both reflects and helps create a balance of energies. Some music is so light and airy that it is designed to open your upper energy centers and enhance your connection to the higher dimensional planes.

There is no judgment in any of this. The full range of music is quite appropriate, and the diverse range of vibrations are extremely effective in accomplishing different tasks. All have their place in your rich reality.

Understand that everything about you is comprised of vibrating energy and is for the purpose of enriching your experience. Some vibrations are created for one sense, like your ears; some for another, like your nose (scents are vibrations, too).

The physicality of your reality here is not solid. Infinitesimal particles of charged light, whirling around other infinitesimal particles of charged light. Their vibration as they travel, the speed, amplitude (depth), and the nature and the number of the minute particles determine the nature of the energy and how it is expressed as matter.

All this is done with intent. Intent is the spiritual 'glue' that binds reality together, that organizes energy into matter and then into experience. This infinite universe and all its dimensional levels are created by the agreement – the intentions – of every consciousness that participates in each level of reality.

This means that you are all the creators of everything you see around you.

You are the masters of this reality, and you each have within you the remembrance of how to do these things. So little of your brains are in use, however, it's not surprising you don't hold these things in your consciousness.

That is changing. At this time you are all being reprogrammed. What an adventure for all of you who have signed up for this time of remembering, of learning how to transcend the apparent limitations of third-dimensional reality and reconnect to the infinite. As your reprogramming takes place and all of your synapses are reactivated, you will be using far more of your brains. You will find an astounding ability to access all that comprises the universe, all the knowledge and experience, all the information that forms the foundation and building blocks of the universe.

And then what an adventure that will be for you.

You each have within you energetics that represent the potential of the entire universe. There are particles representing everything that has been, is, and ever shall be within you, just waiting to be uncovered, waiting for remembrance.

You chose to come here to experience so many great things, so you each are fabulous repositories of awareness, of knowledge and unique perspectives. You are each riches, libraries, abundance, each faces of the infinite God

Life is all about differences, diversity, the intriguing, awesome, almost incomprehensible variety within our universe. The whole creation of the experience of life is because God, who began as the singular intention of beingness, the One, 'split' into many. And, one individual aspect of the One became you.

So, know that each one of you has the God within, and you have chosen your life so you can expand the experience and the understanding of All That Is.

But also know that your brains in these bodies each carry in consciousness but a small part of reality. Most of your brains that are actually in use are simply the repositories of your direct experience here in this one life.

But let us say you have a creative thought, that which is not directed by your immediate experience. This means you have established an ability to break down the barriers within your own mind, and you are accessing that part of yourself that knows how to access the great universe of all thought, all experience.

If you want to be more creative and use more of your brain, raise your vibration, enhance your frequencies. Deal with the handicaps that you have so bravely chosen in this life in order to develop the capabilities of your mind and your spiritual synapses in order to create greater connections with your soul.

You will be amazed at the remembrances that begin unfolding, remembrances of everything from bits and pieces of past lives, to premonitions about the future, to understandings of greater realities and different dimensions. They are all there, the knowledge of all these things resides within you, waiting patiently to be brought into consciousness so you can utilize the wisdom they carry in your daily lives.

How is this accomplished, where are all these riches held inside you? In the fundamental building blocks of your physicality, in your DNA. But not the two strands you once thought; you do not have but two strands of DNA, you have twelve, and they are starting to reconnect. Even your scientists are discovering this. One won the Nobel prize with that discovery some years back.

If everything that defines who you are in this life is contained in the billions of chemical codes stored in your two activated strands, just imagine the information that's waiting there for you to uncover in those ten additional strands. What an abundance of knowledge there. The rest of the universe awaits you... from within.

That reconnection within you is taking place, you are beginning to access it. That is why so many are beginning to be dissatisfied with the status quo and beginning to see possibilities for reality beyond that which exists at the end of your nose, so to speak. As a species, you are starting to actively look for new and unusual ways to explore your reality, your experience, even your spiritual being.

You would not be listening to one such as myself if that were not true. You would, instead, be looking for a great bonfire for this book that you now hold in your hand.

The vibration on this planet is increasing. As it does, you will each be able to access greater and greater parts of yourself, and you as a conscious entity will become increasingly 'new and unusual' yourself. You will no longer be bound by the limited perceptions of your limited experience on this planet. You will each begin to remember astonishing truths from beyond this dimension.

At this point you simply have forgotten all of it. That is why there is so much activity from ones such as myself who have come here to help give you what you need in terms of information and energy. Though what you are hearing is actually of less importance than the energy imbedded in these words, the energetics that are being exchanged in this communication. It is this energy that is reprogramming you at a greatly accelerated rate.

This is why you are being led to us. After each period of communication, after you put the book down, you come from this feeling as though an energetic whirlpool bath has taken place throughout your being. You feel strange, strong, empowered. There might even be some emotional backlash as your emotional selves release some deeply held toxins from an old blockage.

That is excellent. That enables you to get rid of those things that inhibit you, that block the connections between your mind limited by your forty or twenty or sixty years of experience on this planet, and that part of your mind that can access all that possibly can be.

Let us speak of that part.

Every one of you is brilliant. Beyond words.

Every one of you has the power to move this planet on its axis.

Each one of you has the power to ignore your gravity and fly. You just don't remember how. You don't think it's possible.

You know how to manifest a pile of gold bullion in the middle of your room out of the energetics in the air. You know how to stop time and eliminate the distances of space. You know how to do this. (Of course, once you truly remember how to do that, you will not always see the need to do such a thing. Outside of your ego, or your limited personality, what need you of a pile of gold bullion? Think about that before you set on a path just to learn how to do something you will see is so unimportant once you travel that path.)

All that has been happening in your reality has been to help you gain the ability to find that far greater part of you that is your Godself. That is the greatest adventure of all.

So, now you are ready for the purpose of this particular step in your classroom you are holding in your hands.

Imagine that all that is, all that ever has been, shall be, all of the God... everything...is an ocean. A great ocean.

Imagine that you take a glass, a vessel. You fill it with the great ocean that is God, the infinite ocean that is all the infinite energy of All That Is.

Look into the glass and ask what molecule of the ocean within has never been part of the great Atlantic. Which has never seen the Mediterranean, the Indian Ocean. How can you say there is nothing within it that has not once been of the river Nile, nor the Pacific, nor any of the rains that fed all the waters.

All the molecules are fully blended, entwined without separation, seamless. The liquid contains some part of All. The ocean encompasses and accepts all the waters, all the rivers, the seas, the lakes, the rains and blends them into one great body. Nothing is separate. All the parts have once been and will be again the ocean.

The Buddhists in your reality see this. This is why, when they sweep up the sands from one of their sacred mandalas, they pour them into the closest water, understanding that the enlightened energy created by the forming of the mandala thus becomes part of all the waters of the world.

So it is with you. Your identity, your personality, your ego, is the glass that holds the liquid. It is the ocean within that is the Godself within each one of you.

You are also the ocean, you are not simply the glass.

You chose the glass that fits your intentions for this life - you wanted a tall glass, or a little delicate one, or a large one, or a pretty one, or one with cracks that helps you develop a great deal of skill in order to mend it...because you wanted to learn something about the life shaped by that unique glass.

You have all done much, you will do more. But you all can do anything, everything.

Separation is an illusion. You've created separation in this reality to enhance the experience. But you will remember the true, seamless, sacred connection, for you are each part of the All, and you honor the God within by choosing the glass that contains it.

For in doing so, you shape the experience, the journey you travel and with the awareness you gain in that unique vessel, you increase the awareness of the ocean.

Everything you experience goes into the glass. Every win, every loss, every joy, every sorrow. Everything you ever felt, saw, hoped, dreamed, created. Every tear, every drop of blood, everything you ever loved and accomplished. It all goes into the glass.

And when you go back home at the end of your lives, and you pour the richness of all that you have created with all your experiences and your blood and your tears into the ocean, your sacred energy adds to the ocean. The ocean blesses you and thanks you for all you added to the Whole. What a great gift.

And then you get to create a different glass.

So, you need to learn to love your physical bodies, no matter how outside the 'popular' they live, for they are magnificent. The sensations they bring to you...they are teachers, they are shapers, they are repositories of knowledge, they are gatherers of richness, of experience. And in that experience, you learn.

They feel emotions and in that is such awareness. Thank all you experience and all you feel, for they bring you much that adds riches to the ocean within you, that you add to the ocean of the Whole at the end of your life.

You don't want to live boring, puny lives. Feel your lives. That's why you're here - to feel, to, love, to rage, to make war and then learn how better to make peace. To yearn and desire and dream and in that to learn how to create that which you seek. To try and fail and try again and learn improvement and persistence.

To weep alone and search out community and bond in brotherhood and enjoy mixing it up with your compatriots. That's why there is more than one of you. Your choices and experiences and differences make life rich, interesting, fun. That's the purpose of it all.

Life is a joy and a game. If you don't like the rules, change them. That is within your province, for you are the creators. All you need do is to enhance your connection with that part of yourself that remembers. You have each made that choice, and you shall.

Now, a bit about your recent reality where so much has been so continuously difficult for so long. What is the purpose in this? The hatred, the violence, the killings, the rage, the floods, fire, drought, earthquakes. The crushing and the crumbling, and the great floods again. 'Why would we choose so much?' you wonder. Are we cursed? Is an area visited by disaster a victim of 'bad karma'? Is it somehow burdened with a crushing spiritual debt because of a dreadful, sinful history, or the depraved behavior of its residents?

Let go of your pictures of judgments and retribution. The universe doesn't work that way. All is by agreement of those who participate.

There are small agreements between a few people; there are great, vast agreements between great, vast numbers of people. There are many cities and areas on your planet that have been created for a particular purpose, they each represent a focus, a point that magnifies a specific function or helps process a specific lesson in your reality.

The agreement for some massive cities in your world, when they were first intended to be created, was that they would be repositories of all those things precious and dear that people bring to those places from their homes all around the world.

Think about this. People are attracted to some locations from everywhere around your planet carrying, as enormous steamer trunks, all their hopes and their dreams and their expectations for a better life, for an idyllic life, for a richer, more powerful, more successful life. They have put a great deal of energy into all those wishes and they go to a particular city expecting it will help manifest them.

There is a great deal of energy in each place, and it is for the purpose of processing all those pictures people bring to that area from all around your world. No wonder there is so much that clashes with each other. Those areas and those who have agreed to live there process all of that with the fundamental nature of their experiences there. No wonder the energies sometimes feel out of control.

Your reality is not separate from you. The earthquakes within you, as you evolve and grow, are reflected in your environment. The fires that rage within you, as you look at all those things you had at this point considered sacred that you are not reevaluating, they simply outpictured themselves in your reality as fires that swept all who stood in their path. The same with the floods...as though the planet mirrored and magnified all the tears of all your griefs and all your pain as great cleansing floods that washed away all that no longer served.

There will be always areas of change. Always. Each locale within your great planet has agreements in place that shape their reality. Those of you who are moved to live in those places are attracted by the overarching intentions of the area as the perfect stage to facilitate your personal dramas.

But know if you approach your lives – wherever you live – without fear, you will not need to manifest that which you fear. Understand that you do that to prove you can overcome your fears. There are those who choose to participate in an event, and then there are those who change their minds, or choose not to participate, for they do not need the lesson inherent in the experience.

There was a photograph in your newspapers some years back of a home left untouched, standing in the center of all those homes that were burned to nothingness when a great fire swept through those mountains. When researched, there was no advanced sprinkler system that protected the property. No special attention from those who fought the blaze. Nothing that made sense of it. Though perhaps the small fact they were Buddhist might have had an effect. Not that one religion nor spiritual path is more powerful at manipulating physical reality than another, but perhaps the beliefs of those people made their physical goods unimportant, and therefore without need to experience loss in order to learn priorities in their lives. Think on this.

There's a lesson in this, as in all things. What you fear, you will manifest. That which you do not fear, cannot find you. Unless of course you have chosen to participate for another reason.

Do not allow yourself to be traumatized by these events around you. You are not victims of your environment, you are the creators of it. Know that your environment simply helps create the lessons that you signed up for.

If you find yourself in the middle of a great event, it's best you look around and ask, 'Why did I choose this, why such a thing? What do I need to learn from this event?' And then once you've learned the lesson, you do not have to attend the class any more. Truly.

Approach your life with open hands and open minds to catch the richness of it all.

It is a fine place to be...here.

{ 5 }

Naked, in an empty room

YOU HAVE ALL BEEN EXPERIENCING great challenges, much turmoil.

This is a time of testing. But the testing is not that of some judgmental God following you around, this is the time of you testing what is important to you in your life.

You are the master that is holding this great yardstick over you. Sometimes you don't feel you're doing very well, you hold yourself in such harsh judgments. If you could just see your immense beauty, if you could feel the God within you – as we see it within you as a brilliant light – you would never know fear, you would never know pain, you would not need to choose such things.

Everything in your lives is what you have chosen...to bring you gifts, gifts of knowledge, awareness. And your experiences are your own messengers of those gifts. We do not send these to you, we are not the ones who orchestrate your lives. You are. You are the one who orders what you need to assume your mastery.

In this time of great challenge for all of you, you have each been going through all the issues in your lives, one by one: the structures of belief, of feeling, of thoughts, of relationships, of how you express yourself through your work. You have taken this time to look at all these things.

It becomes difficult, painful when you are not very well connected with your soul, when you do not see what no longer works...'This person is not growing, and this job is stifling me, this relationship is stagnating.' You do not see these things so you make no effort to alter or let them go. You resent their inadequacies, you look for those to blame, you stew, you grieve, you rage. You suffer.

So your soul creates the situations in your life that have been, one by one, taking away those things which no longer serve you, which cause you to suffer. But because you are out of communication, you with you, the limited you with the unlimited you, you don't know that you are the ones who asked for these shakeups, these terrible wrenching endings.

All you feel is the pain. This is a sadness to us, for we cannot come in and fix it for you. We cannot come in and take your pain away, as much as we would like to.

We cannot force you to see clearly and easily that which is for your highest good. We cannot make you 'get' it. We cannot even hold your head underneath the water to make you drink - like the horse who, although led to that trough, still will not drink.

We certainly cannot bribe you to let go of one thing with the certain knowledge of the better outcome ahead. That would be like telling a child if he or she would only let go of the lollipop, we promise to give them a chocolate bar in twenty minutes. You must learn to find and understand what is for your own highest good. To bribe you with sure knowledge of the happy ending ahead would keep you as children.

We cannot live your lives and we cannot tell you of every step. That is not our job. That is yours.

We can only give you guideposts and hope that you will see them. We can give you information and hope that you hear it and not think simply, 'It is my subconscious yammering at me. I cannot listen to this, I do not trust it.' You do not trust yourselves because you do not see the face of God within each one of you.

If there is one thing we could tell you that you should feel, not hear, but feel, embrace into knowingness, it is that you are your creator. You are all God.

You have the power to do what you wish, you just do not know it. So, this time has been greatly difficult. You've all had great losses in your lives – relationships, work, things you thought you could not do without. You thought, 'I cannot live without this. I need this.'

You need nothing. You are everything. After you learn that, then you can have it all, because you will understand that you can only create what is already inside of you. We will speak more of this remarkable dynamic later.

Just understand that during this time of clearing your being, all that has been taken from your life has been for the purpose of letting more light in. It has been to make room for that which serves you better.

Think. You came into this life with parents, siblings, companions. You had relationships, you knew disappointment, you didn't get everything you wanted, you sometimes didn't get anything you wanted. And what you got was sometimes not what you wanted at all.

You knew anger, pain, loss, fear – because your life didn't organize itself according to the pictures your child's mind created.

So, you created layers of emotional pain that you stored on yourselves like pockets of tar, and this stifled your reactions further, and buried your connection to your soul further. And with each layer of experience and pain and disappointment, of expectations not met, of pictures never realized, you became layered like a great thorny artichoke.

An artichoke? All prickly on the outside, many layers, a lot of work. You peel and peel and peel and just when you think you're down to the good part, there's the choke.

What you are doing in your lives is peeling back those layers - the prickly ones that hurt, the ones you have created all your lives - of expectations not met, of pictures never painted properly, because you believed in the illusion of separation, of limitation.

You believed life was something that just happened to you, and that sometimes you just got horribly, incredibly unlucky. You believed in good versus bad, in sin and temptation. You believed that evil was lurking around every corner and that if you didn't toe the line you would be flattened. You believed all the awful, judgmental things everyone and everything in your society told you.

You felt that experience had to be gained at a price. You felt knowledge was only gained by difficulty.

You felt salvation had to be bought at the cost of great suffering.

The greatest lie in your reality? No pain, no gain. You believed it had to hurt, so it hurt. A lot.

You created all these prickly layers. What you are doing now, you are pulling them off, one by one. But they hurt, they cause you to bleed...you had put so much energy into creating these layers – based on expectations, based on a lack of understanding of who you are – that they defend themselves with thorns.

The purpose of life is not to suffer, it is not to be somber, it is not to be in judgment of yourself or of anyone else. It is to be in joy, it is to be in love. It is to love every part of yourself and of everyone around you.

This is the time that your planet is being called upon to help raise all of you to a greater reality...so you can let go of your ingrained desire to create sadness in your life through your judgment. You have chosen this time to look at all your painful layers, so you can let go of your own thorns.

As you tear apart the structures of your lives, of those beliefs you felt kept you safe....as you learned the lie behind those talisman, those amulets, those totems you thought kept you protected and somehow validated you...the titles you felt you needed, the attainments you felt you needed to earn, in order to make sure you were OK...you must find a way to come upon an important truth.

You are OK stark naked in an empty room. You need not the trappings that you have worked so hard all your lives to attain.

What has this time been? To show you this ultimate truth: That you, stark naked in an empty room, are perfect.

There is nothing more that has real meaning for you. Once you peel back the layers and you find your heart, in that heart you will find the face of God. And you will know that it is you.

Feel this truth., do not turn from it. We know this truth is frightening because in this truth is responsibility. There is no longer the comfort of wearing the role of a victim as a thorn coat. 'It is not my fault,' the victim says. 'I did not do such a hurtful thing. Life did this to me. I didn't create this. I hurt. I weep. I wail.' So then the victim turns to another, with hands out almost like claws and says, 'What will you do to make me feel better?'

It is hard to give up that role, because when you realize that you are your own God, you are that naked person standing in an empty room, you have to find a way with no trappings, amulets, totems, to be perfect in yourself...to be whole, to find joy, with no vehicles, no jewels, nothing on you, no briefcase, no titles, no beautiful home.

You need not these things.

The Godself within each one of you knows this. So what has that part of you been doing? Patiently, lovingly, teaching your limited self how to move beyond the limitations. You have chosen your lessons to teach yourself that you are perfect, you are complete, you are God.

Once you realize this, you do not have go through all the things you've been putting yourself through – all of these losses you have sustained that have caused you such grief. Some of them have been tangible events, some of them have been losses of belief, in perspective.

We feel your resistance to this - believing you did all this to yourself.

The frightening thing is to go to the heart of yourself and realize there is no place to hide. There is no cavalry, there is nothing outside of yourself. You are the creator of everything in your lives. So own it.

Life is the process of coming to the essence of who you really are. (Repeat this to yourselves a few times...)

In your reality, you are running out of time. But there's much called for, much processing, much releasing, much integrating, and much growth. This is why everything is speeding up, becoming more intense. There is no time to sit, you have to get it now, along with everyone else on your planet. So, your higher self is raising the volume. The time to rest is after you have gotten it.

But it does not have to hurt. Your higher self is not a psychotic demon who wants to flail the living flesh from your bodies. Unless, of course, you think you need such an experience to learn what you will not learn otherwise. See the joy, know that you are who you are and that is infinite. You are God. The whole purpose is for you to take the veils off, to see that.

You do not have to endure artificial constraints to define your mastery. You do not need to suffer to know how to release your crutches, to know that you can choose what you want in your great lives. You do not need permission to see that you can be a sovereign individual in an empty room, without adornment, without anything that marks you as superior to the rest of the world.

Throw those pictures away. We are not saying these things...titles...grand vehicles...opulent clothing...sparkling jewelry...are unserving or inappropriate. We are saying you cannot need these things to prove that you are OK.

You need nothing to validate you. The things you felt you needed to prove to others that you were OK, those are the things you have been stripping from your life with all those wrenching events you created.

Do not feel your pain and ask what you're doing wrong. Do not take that whip and beat yourself further. Take your pain and look at it, and ask what it is telling you. Ask it where you are wounded, where you should look.

Look at your anger, ask it, 'Why am I trying to separate myself from you? What part of myself am I trying to kill with anger? Why do I need the anger to align myself with a belief, to justify what I choose.' Then integrate it, bring it all into your being.

Ask your fear, 'Why am I so uneasy about this part of the unknown, why am I afraid of the lack of control?' For that's what fear is - when there's something not known, something that you cannot control, it creates fear. Ask yourself why does a particular issue trigger your fear, why is it problematic for you, where does it come from, what is it that you cannot bear to happen, what can't you bear to face.

Understand what I am telling you here. Use your emotional feeling states as a detective would, to find out what is going on within you.

It is OK to go to others and ask their input, their advice, their direction. But the ultimate filter is in you. You can listen to twenty people, you may hear twenty truths; but listening to all these people will not tell you what your truth is, only what their truth is. Listen, but then run it all through the filter of your own heart and find your own truth.

Do not worship the teacher, or the guide or the source of information or wisdom. Honor only the lesson.

There are many ways to find crucial information; but remember, you are your own God, so what is true for you may not be true for another. The purpose of your path and everything that you find on the way is to teach you how to be your own teacher. It is to eliminate the illusion of separation between your personality and your soul, between you and others, between you and the rest of the universe.

You are not separate from me, you are not separate from any that are beyond your reality. They're all a part of you. We are all God. You are simply uncovering all of the richness of the universe within you, and then finding what works for you within that.

Trust that it is different for every individual. Feel this. Don't think it. Feel it in the heart of your being. This is where you will find the truths that are yours.

You have spent a great deal of your evolution on this planet trying to figure out what's going on around you, to figure out what you see, what you hear, what you feel. This is excellent, your mind is an exceptionally fine tool. But it is not your engine. Use your mind to observe and to analyze, but do not think that your mind can see all that is.

Your mind is a construct of this reality, a limited mind created by your experience in this incarnation. The trick is to go beyond the limited mind to the unlimited, beyond the layers of the artichoke.

We are not outside of you, nothing is outside of you. This is the great truth. I am not an entity that lives beyond your constellations. The archangels are not in this quadrant, the incarnate guides in that quadrant. Space and distance are illusions, nothing is truly separate from anything else. Beyond the inherent time and space of the lower dimensions, all is seamless.

We are all the ocean.

You want to access everything? That's what this process is about, to get you to understand that you can do anything, access anything, manifest, feel, experience anything you want. You do that by overcoming your belief that you are limited, that you are a victim, that you are not in control, that you are not the creator, that you are not loved.

Know you are loved.

Again, let us say that love is the ultimate frequency of energy, an energy that accepts without condition, it is the sum of all things. Of course you are loved, you are made of this. It is this frequency of energy, the greatest, the core, the grandest building block of all existence. And it is the ability to understand this frequency, to access it within your being and to use it, that will create the life you seek.

There is a point in awareness where one cannot understand everything with your mind. You use your mind to define a thing, and that definition limits it. Think about this.

Defining something, limits it.

You build little walls with words. Some things have no walls, some things can merely be felt, experienced. Use your mind to see what can be, and use your heart to fill in all the rest.

So, this time has been increasingly painful on a very deep level. You think you've gone through the great pain of the great separations in your lives, seeing in front of you those things that had to be taken away. That were. But now you're having to deal with the self that remained after those things were taken away.

And you are now understanding there is nothing outside of yourself.

The lesson is not outside of yourself. It is in the wound that was left behind.

The lesson is not in what has been taken away from you - that you took away from you. The lesson is in dealing with what is left, it is bringing that into wholeness, it is bringing it into awareness, into harmony with the rest of you. This has been the most difficult time of all. Because now you think, 'Dear God, what is left?'

What is left is God. You. That which is you, the naked you in an empty room. That which is the light. That which is the soul. That which is the ennobled part of the face of God. That is you. That which is beyond perfect, that which is sacred. That is what is left.

You are having to adjust to the fact you've let go of all your old, cherished dreams and hopes. You've let go of your crutches, and you stand on your own feet and you begin to take your steps.

This time will be painful in that regard. The energies here are to help you in this process, to look within to see those parts of yourself that are so tender and sore from all you have given up.

But understand that you've really given up nothing of real value. What you have given up has created the potential for a greater reality. You have created potential, not limitation, the possibility of a much more wonderful future.

Use this time to go within. Search out those parts that still bleed and weep within you. Ask them why they are so fearful, why they don't trust they will ever heal. Work on them.

This is a time of preparation, to get down to the essential you. You are not going to get stuck in this great hole forever; yours is not the future of the abyss. You must trust this. The universe is not cruel nor capricious. How can it be…the universe is you.

There is a natural cycle and rhythm in your reality. There are times to go through one layer and another and another in your own artichoke. There will be a time of the healing, and then regrowth; and then you will go through another phase, a transition where you will divest yourselves of even deeper layers of the pain you have built up throughout your lives.

But you can enjoy a time of riches and a time of joy as you embark on the great adventure in front of you.

So pack your bags and set out on your journey, for all is in front of you.

Feel the wind and know that you are that wind. You can go anywhere you wish without limit. Where do you want to go?

{ 6 }

Get out of your boxes

YOUR MINDS ARE AMAZING. They were programmed to give you everything you need to ensure your survival through difficult and changeable environments. And, they are a wondrous window into your creative imagination.

But the problem with your minds is that they think that they know everything. They think they are the engine that drives your existence in this life.

Your culture encourages this belief, sadly at the expense of your other kinds of awareness...your ability to sense emotional states in those around you...your ability to 'know' when someone is being truthful with you...your ability to sense which option among a field of strange unknowns is for your highest good...your sense that you should not go someplace, for there danger lurks. You so seldom feel the connection you share with everything in your universe, the natural connection that allows you to gain energy and insight from everything around you.

You have been trained to so depend on your mental abilities, to analyze and judge everything around you with your mind, to mistrust what cannot be proven, that you have lost the senses of communication and assessment that connect your animal kingdom. Those senses have not really gone anywhere, they have just been so overlaid with your gross physical senses, which have become tools that feed the mind, that you do not hear them. Like a whisper drowned in a bowling alley.

Your minds are great enhancers of experience, but they are not the most important component of your being. Not at all.

As we have said, your mind is the repository of your limited perceptions of that which you have experienced in this one life. You have been trained with your mind to study, analyze, measure, define, judge everything in your reality around you.

The problem with that? What if your yardsticks are too puny, to narrow-minded – literally – to measure the great perceptions, the great potentials...the universe of information...that lay outside of those yardsticks.

You can only measure what you believe already exists. Think about that a moment.

You can only measure what you already know. And the need to measure everything around you ultimately will limit the possibilities of your lives.

Where does knowledge come from, where does expansion come from? It comes from the ability to imagine that which you have not seen. It comes from what you have not yet experienced, what you do not yet know. Not from your ability to bring out a yardstick and hold it up to all that is around you and say, 'Is this valid? Is this not valid?'

By clinging to your yardsticks, you limit your reality. Because what you imagine, you can manifest – if you accept it is within your power to do so.

You cannot manifest what you cannot imagine. Like an artist, you can only create what is already within you.

With your mind, you believe in the validity of something. With your mind, you think that only what you believe is therefore all right to feel. You have it backwards.

What you feel is far more important. That is what you should believe.

And that is why you are here. To feel.

Now, this is a bit misleading. It is not that feeling is the goal, it is the process, the journey. The goal is not to feel pain, anger, fear, and all of those emotions that give you such distress. It is to feel them because they tell you much about yourself and your heart and where you are wounded, where you dislike yourself, where you are afraid of the unknown. They help you see where you need to grow, to heal. And it is your emotional states that tell you what is truly important to you, what makes your heart happy, where your passions lie, what is sacred to you.

What you feel is your reality – not someone else's reality, not your teachers nor your parents, not your friends, or their friends. Certainly not your leaders or your media. Your reality is bound – and unbound – by your reality. Your reality.

What you believe is your attempt to get a yardstick from here, a tee-square from there, pounding down the tent flaps all around this belief in order to contain it and make it safe. To make your lives safe.

But to be safe is to be stagnant, to be stagnant, is to be dead. All that is living is in movement. Understand you this?

Know what emotion is? It is thought that moves you. It moves you to another place of being, another place where you can explore new possibilities, new choices, a new reality. If you do not like the place where it moves you, then move to another place and then another and then another one. But do not stand still.

Life is not about standing still. Life is found in exploring the infinite vibrations of energetic possibilities and what can be created with your intentions. But only if you are willing to move from the old to the new. From yesterday to tomorrow, from here to there and there and there and there. You get the idea. It is only in moving beyond what you already know and are experiencing in the present that you expand your life. It is only through movement that you evolve.

Now, your fine minds bring much discipline and much energy to your evolution; they are a great tool to both focus your attention and expand your perceptions – as long as you don't let them limit what you allow yourselves to see.

You use your mind to look for paths to evolution, to mastery - the most efficient paths, of course, for that's how the mind wishes to proceed. The mind hates waste and dalliance. So you read books, attend lectures, look for lists on how to clear yourself and rituals on how to refine yourself. You search, you study, you ask experts what are their truths and what they think you should do next. That is certainly fine. But do you really want to hang your own evolution on the experience and perceptions and knowledge of others?

A child learns by going to others, and that's appropriate; but then there's a time when the child must grow up and go out in the world in search of his or her own truth. There comes a time when children must use their own experience to shape their own wisdom and find their own perspectives on life.

This is the time when you must do the same. Go ahead, go to others for their insights. But then test those insights in your world, and then go into yourself to find your own truths.

Go to your heart.

What do you feel? Your heart is that which guides the tool of your mind to see the world around you, to see the potentials that exist. But your mind cannot understand that which is not finite. Because your mind is finite. Only your heart is infinite.

Your heart is the connection to all that is beyond the surface of this reality. Your heart is the connection to the infinite universe, to the God that indeed is us all. It is your heart where you will find the greater truth of the infinite library of the universe, where you can access understanding beyond the limited perceptions of those around you. Where you find true inspiration.

Do you understand where creative leaps come from? Not from your linear, limited mind. It takes you from A to B to C very well...that is what it is trained to do. But what takes place when you look from A to B to C and all of a sudden you come up with Q? A creative leap.

You have just transcended the limitations of your limited, linear mind and made the connection to the sacred soul, the doorway to the infinite universe within each one of you.

And in that you have just opened your own 'interdimensional' connection. You have reached the doorway to a higher frequency within you. You have found the river that is within you, the river that connects you with the ocean of the infinite universe.

Know this, know that you are connected to All That Is. You are not, never have been, never shall be alone. The riches of the universe are within you at all times. All the consciousness in the universe is available to you. Because we love you. We are here not only to help, we are here to learn from you, to share in your quest – for your quest is ours in ways it is difficult to explain. And we are always available for your connection, whether it is conscious or not. We are always here to help you whenever it is for your highest good, whenever that sacred Godhead within you calls upon our energies for assistance, and whenever your personality allows.

Allows? Why would you not allow help, why would you not wish for life to be easier? The answer is this: When it would interfere with the path you have chosen to walk in this life; when it would minimize the import of the experiences you wished to know and the impact of the lessons you wanted to master.

You are wondrous because you have committed so much of your hearts and your minds and your bodies unknowingly in this life. You who have been so buffeted by your feelings, over which you felt you had little control. You who have felt the despair of loss without understanding, of anger without context, of pain without the ability to see beyond it.

You ask, 'Why me? Why all this?' And the answer is because you chose this. You chose to learn great truths in your lives and to explore them so that when you go home at the end of your lives, you pour the truths that you carved out with your lives into the great Ocean...adding to it, adding to the understanding of All.

So, in your path to become enlightened, you apply your discipline and your will and you look at your lists and you start by saying, 'I've heard I must clear all my chakras.' So you sit and you think of colors, and you think of vibrations that will help you and you listen to the teachers you hope will save you.

Know what will save you? It is getting outside of the boxes you have built in your lives.

Think of the boxes that form your lives.

Think of the boxes of beliefs – that limit what you trust, that limit what you feel.

Think of the boxes you live within. The boxes with wheels that move you from one place to another.

You live your lives in boxes that have made it easier to live, so you do not have to be quite so buffeted by everything outside of your boxes.

But they limit your potential, too. You begin to think that everything that is inside the boxes is all that exists. So of course you are fearsomely afraid, and you are in pain and sorrow and you think, 'Is this all there is in these little boxes? Who is going to be the cavalry to rescue me from this?'

And so again you look at your books and you come to your teachers and you search for gurus and you ask for knowledge and wisdom. That is why you have picked up this book and peer through every page, studying every word, hoping to find the magic combination that will ease your search and point the way. But our goal here is to get you to the point where you can look to a mirror and see the God in you.

Throw your lists away. Stop concentrating on your colors and your rituals and your breathing. Get outside of your boxes.

Know you what you should do? You chose to be incarnate upon this world, with its wealth and its riches of experience.

When was the last time you stepped foot on the dirt of this planet with your unclad feet and felt its living body beneath your flesh.

When was the last time you stood in front of a great fire and felt the warmth of it wash across your skin.

When was the last time you felt the wind in your face. And smelled the air caressed by newborn blossoms. And felt the stars beating their energy directly onto that crown chakra you concentrate with so much discipline to open to those very star energies.

When was the last time you stood in a place where the light of your cities did not drown out the stars in the night sky, and you looked up and you saw the Milky Way wrap across your horizon like a sparkling veil. You felt you could almost reach up and grab it and embrace it around you like a living, sacred cloak, and feel the love of the universe in your being.

When was the last time you looked within the eyes of a young child. And you saw in this child's eyes the wonder of the absolute innocent, of a being who is completely in trust, and you felt that stir within you in kind.

When was the last time you looked into an old one's eyes, and comforted their fear of what they did not know, their fear of the abyss in front of them.

When did you stand naked and feel the sun, your lover, bring its blessings and its grace to you.

When is the last time you looked into the heart of another being and understood absolutely that you were not separate from that one, that you were one and you felt the heart that you shared with this being. And you loved this other person, not because of what they had done for you, but simply because they were there, and they were another face of you, another face of God.

When did you hear the music of life, feel the rain cleanse your body, feel the heat clear your soul.

That is how you clear your chakras.

You connect with this planet. You chose this home, you are made of the stuff of her great body...she gave you your body. Now the stars, you could say gave you your spirit, but when you go home, your body returns to the body of your mother...a gift in return, a blessing, a communion.

And loving your mother is not just about putting your used papers and plastic in little boxes. It is more than recycling. Loving your mother is stepping outside of your boxes and feeling the oneness.

Trust that she will bring you riches of knowledge, of information, the ultimate feeling of love. She gives you everything, she has given you everything...because you simply are. Sometimes you don't treat her well, you spew your toxins into her body and clutter her beauty with your castoffs. She forgives you. Love her, love being here, love being of her. Honor her, honor that part of you that is her.

There are many on your so-called 'New Age' path that feel somehow the body is lesser, and the spirit is greater. That is foolish, a manipulative perspective by those who have wished to control you in your history. It is hard to control a people who are happy and in joy; and there is little more powerful source of joy than living the connection through your body to your planet with every step of every day.

But we ask you, if your physical body was so gross and unappealing a creation, why would anybody want to come here. It is amazing to be on your planet, to be allowed to feel the weight of your gravity pushing you into the body of the mother, to feel the incredible sensations of experience that your bodies provide here. Be still a moment. Feel the living heart within you bringing you life. Feel the air upon your skin and the light within your eyes, feel each breath and scent and taste and sound. Glory in all of it.

Love yourselves for you are sacred. You are the infinite, you are love made manifest by the marriage of spirit to this earth. You are the children of this.

Honor both. Love your bodies, love the experience your bodies bring to you. They are a great receptor of experience. Do not limit this experience by looking at all the wonder that is around you and saying, 'What shade of blue is that bird?' 'What is the temperature outside? How many miles to our next stop? How fast can we get there?'

Do not analyze your experience, do not measure it. Just feel it. Allow yourself to be. This is a rich place. We've said there's a vast waiting list of consciousnesses who want to be in this place. This is true.

This is not a punishment, the flesh incarnate is not a punishment. The flesh is not a trap, it is not something that if you give into it you are weak or evil.

The flesh is of your mother, and the gift of your mother. It is the gift of your Godself who loved you enough to bring you here, so that you can experience all the riches of this expression of the universe.

Have you absorbed all this? This is how you clear your chakras, this is how you clear your connection to spirit. Do not put your spirit at odds with your body, they are not adversaries. It is only when you realize that such a perceived separation is an illusion, that you will make a great leap on your path.

So love the strengths of your mind, but do not be limited by its perceptions. Your mind is what judges your lives and your world because the mind does not understand that which is outside of its puny, little yardsticks.

Once you are in trust, once you are in acceptance of all that is in front of you, of all that you feel, then you are in utter connection with your being. There is no separation. There is just the moment.

This is what life is. It is a joy. Feel it.

Do not let judgments of any kind interfere with your lives. You all have pictures of what you think rightful living is, you go around judging others constantly. You think, 'They are not as right as I am.' Or you look at someone and think, 'They know more than I do.' And then you judge yourself.

Every time you judge something, every time you assign a number, a value to something, you are building a wall…a wall that will get in the way of your understanding, of your feeling, of your embracing the riches of your reality. You cannot define your reality, and if you try, you will limit it mercilessly.

You can learn to direct your lives where you desire by connecting with your soul. You learn to connect with your Godself by marrying your spirit with your body. And you start by stepping outside of the little boxes in which you have organized your lives.

Life is not meant to be comfortable. Life is meant to be full.

Imagine you are traveling across the country. You board a train...nice, smooth tracks, the air is conditioned, you see everything pass you by through a window. Unfortunately train tracks are essentially straight, it is impossible to take side journeys when something off the structured path attracts your attention. Portions of the sides and possibly the roof are made of glass. You can see all sorts of things as they move by your sight, but you can't smell what you pass. You can't feel the warmth, you can't hear the birds or meet the people. You can't stop when you wish and learn something new.

It is all very sterile, it is all very clean.

It is a pleasant, comfortable journey, but you will have made it to the end of your journey without having learned anything. Because your images are sterile, they come with no feeling, no sensations, you've not touched, tasted or heard anything of the lands you cross. You see only images that your mind assesses and catalogues. It is like watching television.

Don't let this be a terrible metaphor for your life.

You learn by feeling, not by observing. This is the point of all this.

Do not limit your existence by what you observe. Because that is simply an artifact of your limited mind.

To limit your existence by what you observe is the equivalent of being in this air conditioned box and traveling across country. You see the visions, but they have no meaning.

Get out of your boxes, your little silver, conditioned boxes. Know we're also talking about beliefs here, not simply vehicles or dwellings. Do not be afraid to leave the familiar tracks of your life. You will not get lost, though you might get a bit dusty.

Create yourself a life in which you experience it up close and personal, where you get dirty and scuffed and even bruised. This is why you are here, not to cocoon yourself in plastic wrap and breeze across the landscape touching as little as possible.

Some of you might find this somewhat disconcerting. If this threatens you too much, all right...you have to find your own truths. You will leave your safe boxes behind when you are ready.

We are not here to tell you how to live your lives, we are telling you to get involved with your life.

We are telling you, among other things...to learn how to taste and feel, hear and smell, roll in the grass and jump from trees. We tell you that you must allow yourself to cry and scream and laugh. Laughing is possibly the best of all of them.

Laughter...what a wonderful part of your experience. On an energy level, you look like sparklers when you laugh. Laughter transmutes negative emotions into positive energies, pain into joy.

Laughter gets you outside of your boxes. It is the equivalent of standing underneath your canopy of stars and feeling the light on your being as it stimulates those parts of yourselves you've kept dark out of fear...possibly because you accepted someone else's pictures in place of developing your own.

You come to teachers to find the way. We are not telling you that you should or should not do anything; we are telling you that the truth is within you. It is not within what others tell you nor what you observe here. It is what you feel, what you feel...as the result of your own experiences.

Feel what I'm saying, do not analyze it. You cannot nail it down and put it into little gelatin molds. Find the truth here, in your heart. This is where your reality is.

If something doesn't feel right, work on it until you find what does. Find that which feels right for you, and for God's sake – literally – stop worshipping the teachers.

The information here is to trigger within each one of you great awareness, an opening of your hearts, so you can feel your own realities. There are very few universal, uniform truths. There are some. Fewer, far, than you believe.

Truth is unique to the individual, for what you believe becomes your reality. If you do not like your reality, change your beliefs, or throw them away. Operate from your heart. Get outside your boxes.

Clear your heart. Stop this schism between what you feel and what you believe. That is the road to greatness, the path to your soul, the creative, infinite well within each one of you, to the healer, the lover, the mother, the father within each one of you...the child, the totem, the pet...the work, the joy, the treasure. It is all in your heart.

Ask if you're OK with your self. That is what life is, becoming OK, loving yourself without all the accessories you think you need to make you OK, loving yourself because you deserve it, not because you have worked hard and earned it.

The universe doesn't love you because you were a good little girl or boy; we don't love you because you came up with some clever accomplishment, some brilliant phrase. We don't love you because of your hair or your great wardrobe. We love you because you exist, because you are of our hearts. That is why we love you.

In our eyes you are masters and great, indeed. So what we ask of you to is to love yourselves. Look within your heart and step outside your boxes. Hold up that mirror and look at your heart and love yourself. For you are extraordinary. You can do anything...not anything you believe...you can be anything you feel.

Do not limit who you are by what you believe.

{ 7 }

Opening your compassionate heart

WE'VE TALKED ABOUT THE IMPORTANCE of opening up your heart.

You go to your sentimental movies, watch your sentimental stories and think the tears will do it. You read poetry and listen to music and think that will do it. You daydream about the romantic attachments in your life and you think that will do it.

These things are hardly even close.

What it really is to open up your heart is to believe that there is no limitation, that there are no boundaries, there is no separation between you and everything out there.

Your heart is not limited nor bound by issues of a parental or a romantic or sexual nature.

Your heart is the connection between your personality and your soul. Your heart is the doorway between you and the infinite, the doorway between you and all that is possible, between you and all that you have ever been anywhere, anytime. Most importantly, it is the doorway to all you can become.

Once you begin to realize that your heart is not fed by your sentimental moments where you sigh and weep and imagine the happy ending, then you will find unlimited experience.

Your heart is the doorway to the true infinity of all of reality. It is the tie that transcends all separation, all boundaries, all limitation.

How do you open it? You live your life, you get involved, you stop reading and rereading all your little books and sitting in dark rooms practicing rituals and affirmations. It's going out in the world and practicing compassion and empathy and courage and truthfulness in everything you do with everyone you meet. No exceptions, it is not dependent on whether you like or dislike someone, whether they agree with you or whether they can do something for you.

It is time, time to take the training wheels off. You do not have to go to others for guidance. We are here not to tell you what to do; we are here to stimulate you so that you do not need us any more, so that you can become the messengers for yourself and then for the others in your reality.

It is your heart that will help you find how to do this, your heart that will enable you to connect to your greatness. Everything you will ever need will come in through your heart.

It is the doorway through which you can step into any reality you wish.

Through your heart you can manifest anything you wish. You can manifest beloveds from past lives into this one for resolution and for healing. You can manifest lovers who share your heart, partners who share your spirit, friends who share your path. You can create work that expresses your hopes, accomplishment that reflects your dreams. You can manifest every wish, every desire, every dream...if they are heartfelt. You can find all you ever imagined and express all your imagination. Your creativity needs not be bound by little tiny thoughts, little tiny hopes and dreams, it can be as vast as the infinite universe.

So, go out as we have said. Stand on your earth, feel the stars on your body. Look at another being in front of you and see the God within them. See you within them.

How to open your hearts? Stop seeing things that separate you from others. If you dislike something in another person, ask yourself what is it about yourself you dislike so much that you focus on it in this other person. Worse, that you project it onto them, unable to deal with it in yourself.

If you put something in front of you and it gives you pain, ask it where is it rubbing up against some part of yourself. Ask where are you wounded, ask it for guidance, ask your heart for guidance.

Your heart is a great compass. It will point the way to your next step on the path to mastery. Your heart will always lead you true, if you learn to open it and connect to the world around you.

Your heart will help you let go of judgment. What is judgment? It is when you look at something and you think it is outside of yourself; or worse, when you think it is truly inside of yourself and unworthy.

There is no good nor bad. There simply is. Everything that is, exists for the purpose of teaching you something; and if you approach all of your life that way, you will find that all true knowledge comes from your heart. You will find that it is through your heart that blessings come and are given.

Here is a good exercise. Think of the person you dislike most in your life at this time. In your mind, pull this person in front of you and ask why you dislike them so much. Listen carefully to your feelings, they will tell you much about you, what you dislike about yourself, what makes you feel inadequate, what makes you feel such a failure that you turn your head from the realization.

Then, find a way to thank this person for the gift of self-awareness they bring you. You might find that the next time you are face-to-face with this individual, you are far more tolerant of them and they of you.

This is not easy. It sounds good in theory and it certainly sounds good in a dialogue such as this, but to actually do this? Do you find that you prefer not to, that you are actually hanging on to your negative feelings? Why is it so difficult for you to explain – even to yourself – why you dislike that person so much? Are you looking for reasons not to do this? What have you to lose... is your anger or dislike so valuable to you, does it validate you? Does it warm your heart? Nourish your spirit? Are you stimulated by the energy of anger? Or, do you somehow need this person to be inferior so you can feel superior.

If you can let go of all of that, you will be taking a good step toward a fully open heart. You will make significant progress toward your mastery.

Look at those feelings you are most loath to release. You will learn much about your prejudices and your beliefs and those things that limit your potential from everything that make you crazy – you know, the things you are most creative in your excuses not to tackle.

Why are you so resistant to do something? Look at it, ask it, ask it for the insights and awareness that it has for you. Things you dislike are nothing but mirrors of those parts of yourself you have looked at and judged as unworthy, and part of your attempt to make someone else responsible for them.

There is not a molecule in any of you that is not worthy. Believe that if you must have a belief. Believe that. Because there is not a molecule within any of you that does not contain the essence of God. How can that be otherwise? How can you look at a part of yourself and say, 'This is inadequate, this is incompetent, this is silly or stupid or inept.'

You absorbed your parents when you were children, you breathed in their judgments and their prejudices, their weaknesses and limitation. You inhaled their history and their parents' and their tragedies. It is time to let all of that go. Thank them for putting great barricades in front of you to give you the opportunity to exercise, to grow the strength to overcome them.

You have more knowledge of yourself because of things you had to work for, than things you took for granted.

This is a truth in your reality, this is a truth in all reality.

Do not judge anything. A judgment is a belief that something is separate from you; and that belief enables you to see it as inferior or superior to yourself. This means you cannot perceive yourself as being 'one' with it. Separation will inhibit your potential for your mastery by limiting how much of your reality you embrace.

It is the ability to view the world through your compassionate heart that will help you find your limitless connection to the infinite universe. It is through that where you will fully remember who and what you are and assume your mastery.

Know that a tiny heart opening sees the world through tiny pinholes. It creates a mean-spirited mind and a mean-spirited being. It takes a large, wide-open heart to see a vast, infinite world.

Sadly, people find this uncomfortable. If you approach the world with your hearts wide open, it is a bit risky is it not. To let others in, to let in all that they feel, to let in all that you feel is a bit too vulnerable for some.

Where is the safety of distance, where is the safety of separation. Where is the protection of all this space.

Why do you need this protection? Think about this.

To have a wide open heart does not mean you're vulnerable to pain, it means you're vulnerable to joy. Do you see the difference? If you are in joy, and you go into the world with no boundaries, no walls, you need no protection. You only hurt where you have separation illusions within you, you only hurt where you are wounded and you haven't healed that part of yourself and brought it into the light.

Think of a pure beam of light. In your mind, imagine it in front of you. See a big, glorious beam of light as a great glowing candle and feel it warm your face, your skin. Breathe this light in and feel it fill your lungs and warm your heart.

Now, does this light have any walls? Does it have any barriers? Does it need any windows or doors? Does it need any protection from the darkness? Does it need armor? Or guns? Or defenses of any sort? Does it need lipstick? A better wardrobe? Bigger salary?

Light is infinite because it is fully open. Do you understand this? This is the greatest truth of all.

Look at the lesson of light. It is infinite, open all around…above it, below it, from every side. Its protection is that it is fully in and of the light. There is no part of it that is dark, it fills the darkness around it. What needs it of protection. Nothing can harm it, it is infinite. Even your scientists know this, light is never destroyed…it simply goes on forever.

That is the lesson of the light.

So, when you think you need your walls for protection against a world that is cold and callus and fearsome and uncaring, think of the lesson of the beam of light.

If you are the light, what need you of anything else. Light does not look upon itself in judgment and say, 'This ray is not nearly as vivid as that one.' There is no separation of one ray from another. 'Why do you go one way? That one is going another?' It simply is.

It is that wholeness which you must learn to find within you. You do not have to work hard, concentrating with focus and great determination to create that light.

The light is everywhere and is everything. You must work to let go of the barriers that you have built up all around the light that is you, the barriers that block your light and diminish its power.

This is the time in your reality to start chipping away at the bricks and the boulders, putting away the chain mail, letting go of the helmet, the shield. That which can truly hurt you will not be stopped by your armor, anyway.

There is nothing you need to fear within the light. You need no other protection from the light. You will find no judgment in the light, no anger in the light, no fear, no pain, no grief, no sorrow.

You will weep, but you will weep from the joy of the infinite connection when you go out onto your beautiful planet. When you smell the day after the rain, you will smile in joy at the great world this is. When you pick up a crystal and you see how it accepts the light and bends it and blesses it, you will be warmed by the lesson. When you look into the eyes of people with all of their greatness, you will glow with empathy, and know that the connection you share with each one of them is this infinite light.

You can look at your enemy, the one whom you feel has harmed you so greatly, and you will be able to understand that the reason why they have harmed you is because they are trembling in fear from their own deforming armor. You will pity them and in that you will find a way to open your compassionate hearts much more. You will look upon them in acceptance, which is a face of love.

That is how you open your hearts.

Once you do that, you can look upon the world and find the courage to drop your own armor. The more you can do that, the more you will be in joy. Do you understand this? This is a simple lesson, but an important one.

If you want an exercise (you like exercises, we know this, they make you feel you are doing something productive), every time there is something in front of you that stirs an emotion that is not joy, think of the example of this beam of light.

Imagine...you are looking at someone who has just criticized your work. Look them in the eye and see behind their eyes that beam of light, look them in their soul and see the light that is within them. Know that the rest is simply armor, and that it is the armor that is their handicap, their sorrow.

Love their light, have compassion for their armor, and simply choose not to react to it. After awhile, they will be more able to drop their armor and open their heart to you if they are able.

Someone has to start first. When you are in the light, is it not easier for you, who have some understanding of the dynamics of this, to do it first? Where is the risk in such a thing. When you lay down your arms, what does the other one do? They have no need to keep holding theirs; it is a burden, and it is hard to do anything when you're holding swords and guns all the time.

They may be slow; with all this armor, it is hard for them to move. We understand the difficulty in this. You lay down your arms first and they might think, 'Well, I might get a free one in.' So they take a shot. Accept it, it will strengthen your compassionate heart. Know that the light will deflect all, and then forgive them. That will strengthen your compassion even more.

When you still do not pick up your gun and fire back at them, they will think 'This isn't any fun at all.' And they are less apt to do it again. Even if they do? Still, deflect it. Use your light to deflect the arrows and the insults away. They cannot hurt you.

Where is the risk in putting your guns down? Think about this.

What do you risk? Pride? Ego? Why must you prove yourself to anyone, what reason does a whole, joyful person have to prove themselves to another? There is no reason to. There are many rich lessons in your Christ legacy. Turning the other cheek is one of the greatest.

You, in the light, are infinitely protected. You can cope with anything, you can heal anything, you can transmute anything, you can process anything. You can process some fool who is standing in front of you, you can help them let go of their armor. Is it not worth a moment of discomfort to be in the light and in your full power? Is it not worth that?

If you are going to risk something, risk that part of yourself you do not need. You do not need anything that keeps you separate from anything or anyone else. Do you understand this?

If you are in the light, if you are like that beam of light, happily glowing away...warming all, infinite in its power, accessing all it can ever possibly need, giving all it has to anyone who comes to it, knowing that it cannot possibly ever be drained – because what it gives is infinitely replenished, and in truth the more it gives, the more it is given – what do you risk?

Drop your armor. In doing that you become the role model to allow others to drop theirs. And imagine everyone dropping their armor everywhere...what a grand idea.

Let the earth absorb it, that's what she does best. She has spent millennia absorbing all those things in your lives you did not wish. Think about that. Think about that again.

You worry, you think you're poisoning her. She has accepted your detritus, your mistakes, and at the end your bodies. She has accepted your excesses and all of those manifestations of your civilizations and your passions and your hatreds and your fears.

She has accepted it all with love, processing it all with love. With love. Because that has been her joy.

What harms her to accept your runoff in her rivers? She trusts you will learn to do better, you will look around and see what you have done. She puts her barriers down, risks a small, little bit in a small piece of time in her vast wholeness of being.

Because she has no pride that requires proof. Hers is the truly open heart.

Your earth is a fine example for you to emulate. She, indeed, turns the other cheek and says, 'I will let my children see the results of their mistakes. I trust they will learn from them. I risk this in love. The river will flow, the ocean will clear, the land will be reborn, and so will my children.'

She trusts you will grow up before you are capable of irrevocable harm. At least, that is the hope. And hope, after all, is the keystone of love.

So...be the earth. If someone wants to dump on you, as you have been dumping on your earth so long, what is the harm in just once not dumping back, simply accepting it, transmuting it. Put your armor down, put your guns down, be as your gracious earth. People will stop dumping on you; for they only dump on things that make them angry.

When someone looks on others with a compassionate heart, where is the trigger for the anger? Think on this. Think on this again.

Be that light, be your magnificent earth.

There is so much in your reality that is truly fine. Your bodies, your skin. Nerve endings...what excellent inventions. The information they give you, the pleasure, the interaction with your rich reality that they allow. Do not let yourselves be so filled with the blur of details and deadlines that you cannot stop for a moment and feel the simple pleasure of something that is cool to swallow, or warm to the touch. Your reality has many wonderful sensations that make your lives exceptional, if you would only stop and notice what you are experiencing as you stumble through your days.

Everything you need to do to tune your bodies up, you will find in your daily existence. Stop and allow yourself to feel all that is around you in all that you do. Feel it in every part of your being. Look around you at the riches everywhere. Is not your planet beautiful in that which she takes from you and accommodates in order to teach you how to be more evolved, more joyful?

Think what you can do for others around you. You can accommodate them and take what they give you and teach them to be better, too.

Be your gracious, loving earth. And in that, what great growth you yourselves will learn. You will look upon all around you in compassion and acceptance, helping them to be better versions of themselves. And, you will look around you, at your lovely planet and understand it is not simply your home, it is you. And you will treat it with love, as it has treated you since time was young.

{ 8 }

What you believe, you live

THERE ARE GREAT WAVES OF ENERGY that are being sent through your reality for the purpose of helping you evolve.

There are times when great energy shifts bring different issues to your attention that you have not yet dealt with – both on a personal and global level.

Know that each period of energy is for the purpose of facilitating different processes in your evolution.

There are times for clearing, to remove the emotional, belief and physical structures that no longer serve you. Imagine a tree letting go of its old, dried-up leaves to allow room for fresh new growth.

There are times for evaluation, for going within to assess the damage left by earlier experiences. Imagine a bear hibernating in a cool, quiet cave. It is the time to look inside your being and see what is left; to look at your poor, wounded landscape, to see the sadnesses, the tender spots, the places where you were still bleeding.

This is the time to tend your fields, to look at the fertile ground of your soul and decide what you want to plant there, what you were making way for with all of your pain and your discomforts, your sadnesses and losses. This is the time for you to decide what you want to grow – that which you want to enfold into your being, what you want to make way for in the future.

When you grow up holding onto all your packages and burdens – your baggage – of beliefs and prejudices and expectations and judgments, you have no room in your arms when the universe throws you something better, something that will expand your perceptions, your world.

In times of clearing, you chose what you wanted to be pulled from you. The trouble is, your conscious self wasn't always in on the decisions. Your soul, yes, but because you have not been in good touch with that sacred part of yourself, you were deaf, dumb and blind, and did not know what was going on. So, it was quite painful. But you chose it nevertheless, and we acknowledge and commend the courage of the choices you've made.

So, you prepared the field. What didn't serve you, what was worn, outmoded, what had become toxic, harmful, you arranged for experiences that would clear to make room for the seeds of the new life that you wanted ahead of you.

And then, the energy shifts once again, and it moves to growth, to fresh beginnings, the time for your seeds to begin opening, the unfolding of all the hopes and wishes, all the intentions that you have for your future.

You may find yourself staring at some little bud, 'Why aren't you opening?' This is the time to learn patience, for in the first day of spring the flowers do not open with a mighty flourish. They take their own time, until each is ready for its awakening.

It's not that time cannot be broken or compressed, it's just there is inertia in time, and it takes its own time, so to speak. But do not think that there is nothing going on because you see nothing happening. Think for a moment about the lesson of the bud. When it opens in a great glorious flash of velvet color, you can see the unfolding of all that had been happening below the surface, below your perceptions.

Before we speak more on the unfolding within your larger reality, let us reiterate some ideas we have so far discussed. Repetition may be somewhat irritating, but trust that the encoded information within this text is presented in such a way to help you unfold with the greatest possible results when it is your time to do so.

We've made it clear that what happens on your earth is not separate from what happens within you, the universe does not start at your skin and proceed outward. You, your universe, are all one. What moves within one, moves within all. All. You are changing, you are transforming, you are transmuting the old selves to make way for the new. So is your planet. The vibration is being raised incrementally.

Now understand that because not all on your planet are as enlightened as others, and not all parts of you are as enlightened as the rest of you, there are areas that are lighter, brighter, there are areas that are darker, denser. During these great energy waves, think what is likely to happen when energy pushes into things that have a different capacity for movement. Earthquakes. Raging weather. Violent upheavals.

What you see happening around your planet at this time are the dynamics of the energy transforming itself in your reality. You are not separate from your planetary system, you are one organism, you each reflect the other.

So, how to deal with the changes that are in front of you. There will be more violent manifestations of the energy shifts on your earth, far greater than you have seen. There are many agreements in place at this time for such events around your world.

This does not mean an agreement cannot be changed. However, also understand that the more individuals who choose to participate in an event – there are physics to metaphysics – the harder it is to form or alter an agreement. It is like getting your Queen Mary to turn quickly; certainly she can turn left...if you give her enough room. There is much inertia in third-dimensional reality; the more people involved, the more energy it takes.

How to protect yourself? Will there be a great event in your locale? What can you do?

Pay attention to what you believe. There were some in Los Angeles and San Francisco who were so convinced there would be a killing quake, that when an earthquake did hit...for them it was.

For them it was. Think about that.

But think of all the others who were not harmed. They had not chosen to participate, they had not bought into that picture, they had not bought into that belief. So, for them, it was not the 'big one.'

Two people, living side by side in two dwellings; one believed one thing, one believed another. One home crumpled, one home untouched. Same event, different outcome. Why did the earth move here and not there. We could say this person chose it, that person did not; though it would be only partly correct, depending on what part of the person you thought had the power to choose. What is more correct is to say that the first person had internal energetics – schisms of some sort – that helped create physical schisms of great velocity in their immediate environment; and the other person had not.

It is a great argument for creating more harmony in your being.

You see, you can control your reality. Again, remember our story of the great fires in a city – great blocks of homes were flattened, blackened. One house in the middle, left untouched. That one did not need such destruction, they did not need such an event in their reality. Maybe they did not need anything to point out such potential destructive turmoil within themselves. Maybe they did not feel the need to participate in the drama of the event. Maybe they wanted to experience the event up close and personal, but still as an observer. So for them, the effects of the fire did not happen.

You are not at the mercy of forces beyond your control. You choose your own reality, your own lessons, your own outcomes.

This is a hard concept for you. You might call it luck, fate, something out of your control. But to be clear....it is not your personality who creates your reality, it is your soul. And your soul may have no use to participate in such an event. Or, it may choose to do so for reasons of its own...as we've said, for reasons of opening your compassionate heart, or of being a beacon in the middle of the event to help those around you, or to use it to leave this existence. You might not know the reasons your soul picks something, but you can eliminate the need to experience it in order to overcome the fear or pain or anger your personality clings to.

Of course, if you find it great comfort to hold onto your old beliefs rather than change them and trade them in on better ones, by all means, hold on to those old beliefs and watch your house fall down the hill. Is that not a great comfort?

Do not be afraid of changing what you believe. We know this is a great fear, but look at the alternative. Do you wish to believe that the universe is a cold, random place, at the mercy of chaos and coincidence? Do you wish to believe that excrement happens? Do you wish to believe you have no control over your reality? Do you wish to believe you do not have control over your destiny?

You say it is hard to believe in that, to believe that you shape and control your world and the events that surround your life. It is hard to believe in that which your scientific thinking has not justified.

It is hard to believe that I – a star being from another system who came and lived many lives on your planet – can so easily bend all the laws of time and space (as you know them) to actually come here and talk to you.

And it is hard to believe in those from the angelic plane. It is hard to believe in the myriad of 'invisible' entities who crowd your reality – your guides, your other, grander selves, your other-dimensional realities, those who have come here from other realities to be of service...all faces of God...all faces, indeed, of yourself.

It is hard to believe in that which you do not see?

Think of the alternative. Believe what you choose, and what you choose will determine your reality.

Is it safer to hold on to your old beliefs? That the world is cold and random, that there is no one here to help you?

If you believe that the world can be measured with little yardsticks, and put in compartments, and there's no one who loves you, and you are at the mercy of everything...then you are the victim of everyone and everything. You have no place to turn, you have no solace. Is that a fine belief? Does that comfort and validate you?

Is it not easier to believe that in the middle of your room there is a great pink angel that is smiling on you? You squint and say, 'I cannot see it, how can I believe in that which I do not see?'

So, instead, you believe in earthquakes that can crumple your home and there is nothing you can do to change that.

Why hold on to an idea that removes all your power to fix anything.

Let us talk about beliefs, how much your beliefs shape your reality. Let's say you drive your vehicle to an intersection, there are cars coming from either side. What a possibility for a great crash. But because you look up and you see a little green light, you do not hesitate, you continue. You believe others will follow by the rules, so you keep on going.

You all share that belief and everything works. This is called mass social consciousness.

Your lives are shaped by beliefs in ways you literally cannot imagine. Because most of your beliefs, you don't even know are there. Society has created this incredibly complex belief system that runs your world.

There are beliefs that have been built up layer and layer upon layer throughout your lives from when you were nothing more than a gleam of light in the eyes of your parents. As soon as you were conceived, one cell to the other, you began to be bathed in an energy field that was shaped by beliefs of all of those in the reality field you had chosen to enter.

Everything you experience has taught you beliefs: Look both ways before crossing the street. Do not do that, you might fail. Do not try that, you might fall down. Don't risk that, you might hurt yourself. Don't trust that one, they might hurt you. Beware of the dark. Open the closet door, there might be a boogieman. If you're not good, Santa Claus won't reward you. Don't go outside, bad people are waiting. Why try so hard, it doesn't do any good. I'll believe it when I see it. And so on…

All of you have heard those things growing up, things that make you afraid of the unknown, untrusting of other people, uncertain of your own abilities. You hear these often enough and you believe them.

You learned to live in a world that is bound by your fears, by those around you. You do not trust; you do not trust the universe, you do not trust yourself. So how can you believe in a benign universe designed to help create what you desire.

And again we ask, what is the alternative? To believe that the universe is a friendly, responsive place, that loves you greatly, that loves you without condition, that we are here to help you, to point the way, to make things smoother, lighter, brighter.

If you believe that, where is the risk. Where is the risk?

You have everything to gain and nothing to lose – except all of those dreadful beliefs that terrify you, that make you afraid, that make you live outside of trust, that make you not trust yourselves. The last is the worst.

When you were stripped of your ability to trust the universe, you were stripped of your ability to trust yourself. For then you believed you were a victim and that you are at the mercy of those who had power over you.

Of course, understand that it has been in the best interests of those who wished to have power over you to make sure you believed you were powerless. Also understand that as creators of your own experience on earth, you allowed this to happen, because you wanted the satisfaction of overcoming great obstacles. An intriguing thought is it not.

So, you allowed yourselves to be deaf, dumb and blind and in such limitation that you believed you were a victim.

But now it is time to uncover the veils and to see that you are the creator of your life, and to then set about determining the kind of reality you seek consciously.

Think about how you can grow a garden that is much more pleasant and productive to live in than what you have lived in thus far. Think of all the pain and sadness and loss you have undergone, as simply weeding your garden. This is not to say that what has been taken from you has no value. It has great value, for it has taught you much about yourselves.

Each person and situation that has been in your life has been much like a class you decided to experience, a lesson you signed up for. When you mastered the lesson, when you graduated, it was then time for the class to be closed. So... friends left, jobs became unpleasant or boring, money dried up. You were forced to move, you were forced to change, you were forced to give up all that was familiar, comforting.

It was just to make room for a far better life.

If you want to believe one thing that will change your life, believe that. Believe in the 'pink angel' smiling down on you.

Is that not a much finer belief that empowers you far more than believing you could step outside your dwelling and be hit by a truck...something you have absolutely no control over. Or there will be a great chasm in the ground that will open up and swallow you whole. Or that a flood will wash your car, your home, your body down the street.

You can control your lives. If there is nothing, nothing you hear other than this, this is enough: You are the creators.

Ok....so now you ask, why in heaven's name did you create a life like this? 'If I was going to create a life, it would be far more pleasant than this. Money would not be a problem. Work would not be a problem. Love would not be a problem. Nothing would be a problem.' Well, how boring would that be and what would you learn?

Do you know what makes a good story?

First, you create people you care about.

Then you set a goal for them to accomplish, something the audience can identify with, but perhaps something that is not entirely clear to the hero until late in the story.

And then you create difficulties in their way. Enemies that confuse them. Frailties that confound them. Obstacles that all but overwhelm them.

So the audience cheers for the hero, for their courage in the face of trauma and their resilience in the face of failure, for their nobility of purpose and even for their weak, sad moments when it seems they will fall and succumb to despair. And then...the glory of the accomplishment in the face of all the trouble and travail. Finally, as the hero looks back at everything, the quiet joy in feeling the power in being able to create the happy ending after all the hardship.

A good story, is it not?

First, the caring. Then the challenges. And finally the growth, the enlightenment, the joy.

No matter what story you enjoy – whether in your books, your movies, your myths – that is the formula. Even those that do not have the picture-perfect happy ending, the ending is still one of enlightenment on a path leading toward the joy.

You are the creators of your own lives. Would you not have picked something as interesting for your own story?

You who have lived so many lives, if you would choose to live the same life over and over and over again in fantasyland, you'd get tired, bored, stupid. You'd learn nothing, and you'd say, what is the point?

So instead you say 'I am a clever person. I care about myself. In this life I want to accomplish great things. So how do I prepare myself to accomplish great things? Well, I have to start with small things. Like jumping over that bar. But first, I have to exercise and become strong.' And so you jump over the bar and you look around and say, 'Well that was fun, now I think I'll raise it a peg.' So now you have to be stronger, and you jump over that bar. 'All right, now. I want to do it again.' And you raise it again.

Your lives are exactly this: training to jump over your bar and then raising it for the next round, over and over and over again. Because if it would stay down at the bottom, low, easy, you would be bored silly and what is the purpose of being incarnate other than to enjoy your lives, to enjoy a really good story.

Think of the hero of a wonderful story, think of the one who slays all the dragons and saves the village. It's not particularly fun while fighting for your life; it's frightening and dangerous and you have everything to lose. But when you're victorious, you get to look back and say, 'Was I not grand! Did I not learn something fantastic in doing that.'

Well, what you are doing here and now is slaying your dragons.

You are the creators of your stories, you are the starring role in each of your lives, you are not the victim of anybody. Do you understand this?

You are likened unto the director, we are the ones who are the producers. We do not direct the action, you do; we bring you the resources to do it. It is simply that the you that is of flesh and blood, the you that you've chosen to be in this life – your personality, your ego – has so immersed itself in your story that you have lost connection with your soul, you have forgotten who you really are.

Over all of your lives you have forgotten much, but this is the life you have chosen to connect with it all. This is the life you have chosen to attain an awareness of all you have been and are and can do. This is the life you have chosen to overcome whatever it takes to achieve that goal, and this is why your lives now are filled with so many dragons.

This is so you will become strong, mighty, filled with the power of your infinite self. If you are challenged enough, you will finally remember that you can access a reality far beyond the apparent constraints of this third-dimensional stage, 'I can call the prop man in to help me....I can rewrite the script, call special effects, change the story!'

But know that no matter what your own personal story is, the final lesson is still...always...to remember that you are a sacred face of the infinite God, and to be in trust in the truth and the power of that.

So, if you do not believe in a pink angel, if you feel that the world is a callous and unfeeling place, and nothing, nothing in your lives has been able to disabuse you of that, ask yourself this: What do you think that you, as your own creator, would be willing to create to move you to the point where you will finally say, 'I have no choice other than to believe in something better, because everything in front of me hurts too much. It is too awful to believe that this is all there is.'

You see, the more you resist this belief, the worse you are creating your reality to make you so exhausted and heart-sore that you will believe it because the alternative is too awful.

We are not doing this to you. You are the directors, you are the screenwriters of your own lives, you chose what you came here to learn. You determine the degree of difficulty. We oblige. We bring you the energies; we work backstage to help arrange all of the agreed-upon events ordered by of all of those who participate.

To make all this easier...just trust in spirit, trust in yourselves, trust in the universe, make that leap of faith. Your lives will become much more joyful, because you have lost the need for the lessons to bring you to that point. You have nothing to lose except your pain.

You want proof? What proof would satisfy you. Look at the proof of your lives so far, look at it all. To believe in nothing, has that given you comfort?

You look to the scientists and their little yardsticks to prove your reality. They cannot even agree among themselves. You look to the theologians, and ask them to define your spirituality. They cannot agree among themselves. God knows the politicians cannot.

So, with no one in your reality in agreement on anything, why not decide to trust in what you want it to be.

You look outside for validation; there is none. No one can validate anything outside of themselves anyway. It is what you believe. If you look for symptoms of that which is truth, think on that one lone house – in the face of all your ideas of reality – standing untouched in a sea of blackened buildings. Is that not proof.

There are things that happen all the time, all the time, that cannot be explained by your limited views of the universe.

Coincidence? Is that a more comforting belief than a loving guidance? It is your choice.

So, when the earth changes sweep your reality, know they are simply reflecting the schisms within you. Hold onto your belief in the angels. If you do not need to participate in those changes, write them out of your story. If you do not need an event to learn a truth, you do not have to live it.

Nothing is random, nothing simply happens. It is all by agreement. And there is no harm in simply choosing to accept that. You have nothing to lose.

You are rich, all of you, and your lives can be beautiful. They do not have to be based on all those fears and all those stories you were fed as children, that the media feeds you, that the experts, the scientists, the politicians, the theologians feed you.

Be your own source of knowledge, of guidance. Trust yourself, you have nothing to lose, everything to gain. A leap of faith can put you in a position where you will learn how to fly.

That is what you are for. And we are here to help you.

Know there will be some fascinating twists in your future. All of your stories are about to become more interesting than ever before. Know you the Chinese curse, 'May you live in interesting times!'?

If you approach your lives with the right attitude, the right intent, you can enjoy them. You do not have to participate in the 'interesting' lessons that will surround you with increasing frequency and intensity. You can simply enjoy your own story – if you trust, if you believe.

Believe in this. Believe in yourself.

{ 9 }

Clearing out the dark rooms, letting in the light

A SEED IS BLOOMING WITHIN YOU. Of self-awareness, remembrance, power. Of enlightenment.

You who have been drawn to this book are now being exposed to energies within these words, activating energies to help you feel an expansion of your senses, a sense of connection to things and times beyond your immediate.

The difficulty is the expectation that as you begin increased awareness, you might think, 'Oh good, my life will be perfect from this time forward. I will not know sorrow or loss, or sadness, or fear. I will not be angry at my mother, disappointed in my mate. I will not be in fear of that which is in front of me that I cannot see. I will finally be totally, completely happy!'

You feel when you begin your 'wake up' that life will become perfect, easy. Unfortunately it is not so.

The moment you begin to wake up...that is when you look around as though you have lived your life up to that moment in a dark room. At that moment, the light turns on and you see that you are surrounded by things that you have collected all of your life – your relationships, your work, your style of life, your friends, attachments, beliefs. All your 'stuff.' And you might not enjoy what they now say about your taste. Or your maturity for that matter.

So you look around this room and you think, 'How could I possibly have chosen that couch? It is hideous. And that lamp...what was I thinking?' You see the friend who did not honor you, the mate who abused you, the boss who usurped you and you think 'How stupid was I? How childish.'

After seeing what you surrounded yourself with, you are harsh with yourself and judge great parts of yourself as being inadequate for having made such wretched choices. And in that judgment, you turn from what could be a great and glorious moment in your evolution.

You could instead look upon all those things with love; perhaps with amusement, but certainly you need to look upon them with kindness, as you would look upon a collection of bright bottle caps and pretty string that a child had collected as it roamed its playgrounds. In that moment, you would be opening your arms to the child you had been and accepting it for all it was, and loving it for having grown up enough to see childish things for what they were and now desiring more appropriate things in its life.

How to do that? Look around your room filled with all these things that you have lovingly, though somewhat blindly, been collecting all your lives. Look at them next to the 'you' you wish to be, next to the future you wish to know, the joy you wish to feel.

Say, 'I do not need to cling to this any longer, but I acknowledge the fact that it gave me pleasure before. I do not need to hold onto that, though I honor the fact that it comforted me before. I can let these things go without judgment, and with gratitude for the service they offered me in the past.'

Let them go with joy, but let them go you must.

If your room is so filled with all of these boxes and lamps and furniture you've collected all your life, there will be no room for anything else. So look at them with new eyes. If they no longer reflect what you care about and value, if they no longer serve you, let them go. People, work, feelings, desires, emotions, relationships, careers, beliefs…let them all go.

You will experience career shifts, there are many of you who are desperately unhappy with what you have done all your lives. If the professional structure of your lives no longer serves you, for it reflects an old you, and there it lurks in the corner of your dark room...let it go.

Your room is piled high with all of these things you thought you could not live without in your life in order to feel ok – the things that you bought because your parents felt you should, your friends felt you should, your child-selves felt you should.

Where is the room for the beauty that is in front of you with all this clutter around you.

The energy waves that have been sweeping through your reality have been to facilitate the release of these burdens, to get you to release your sticky little fingers and let go of your old toys and clear your rooms.

That is what a child does; it holds onto something with sticky little fingers for dear life. They cannot do without that security blanket, that teddy bear, that shiny red bike, the car, the lettered sweater, the promotion, the mansion, the beautiful mate...it goes on and on through the years. The toys simply become larger and more showy.

You could not live without that chair, and now you look at it, 'Oh dear, if I let go of this, mother will be crushed. If I turn off that lamp, how will I make my living? If I let go of this carpet where will I warm my feet at night?' Well, look around at your room and ask yourself how happy are you now.

All these things have not brought you joy, have they? You bought them because you felt they would bring you comfort, you thought you could purchase your safety by buying all the little pictures in all the magazines and collecting all the things that other people projected upon your souls. Let go of them.

When you stand there, with your hands empty, your room clean and bright and sparkling, that is when the universe can bring you things that are far more suited to you now. But when you are so burdened down and cluttered by all of this foolishness, of childhood things you thought you could not live without, of beliefs that create a reality in which you know only disappointment – beliefs that interfere with the connection with the God within each one of you - we ask you this...where's the joy in your life?

When is the last time you felt warmed by your sunrise? When is the last time you looked into another's eyes and felt that intimate connection with their God within them, and you felt their regard equally for you?

This is what life is all about, not about collecting all of these things, and pieces and parcels and boxes. They do not make you happy, they certainly haven't so far.

What makes you happy is exploring who you are without all of the silliness and the trappings and the burdens and the armor, it is exploring the God within you.

Let go of the things that you place around you as a castle – or a fortress – to protect you from an unfeeling world. Let go of the playthings that you use to distract you from the emptiness you feel in your lives. Find out who you are and what is for your highest good, explore your world, your lives, your soul.

You start by paying attention to everything.

Pay attention to your life, pay attention to all that you placed around you, to the people, the events – large and small – you have created, to the roads you have walked, the destinations you have reached, the goals met, the goals unmet. Look at the wins, the losses, the things you hate, the pleasures that make your heart happy. Look at all you have done and what you feel undone in your lives.

You are not passengers on this train. You told us where to put the tracks. You told us. We simply facilitated your desires.

We were there with our hammers and glue guns, but you chose your lives, because you wished to learn something new. This is why you've chosen all of your lives.

Remember, you choose your lives because you wish to learn something. Each life you have chosen is for the purpose of helping you understand a different aspect of being that interested you.

Now, once you've chosen your life, know that all is not written – some is, some choices you have made, but far fewer than you believe. You have the capacity to direct your lives, especially at this time in your reality when the rules are open-ended.

Reality is changing, time is changing. How many of you have been experiencing time shifts lately? All of a sudden, you looked up and wondered where did all that time go? Or you were extremely busy and accomplished a vast amount of things, and you looked up and noticed only twenty minutes, that is all that had passed.

You are the ones who are learning how to change the quality of your time, you are learning how to bend the reality in which you find yourselves. That is your ability, that is your heritage.

Understand that part of the purpose of the great energy waves is to bring you new possibilities, new tools to facilitate your evolution during this time of the transition. As the waves bring in new capabilities, you will find yourself participating in many strange and fascinating phenomena.

But also understand that you are not alone in this time, for all beings in all dimensions are now coming to a time of quickening and of growth. We continue to grow, just like you. One does not attain a particular level – or dimension – of being, of vibration, and then sit there like a mushroom for the rest of existence.

This is a time of quickening, and for all to become more, better, bigger, greater, grander, brighter. We are all working to shine, to hold more of the infinite light, the light that is the core building block of all reality.

All of the energy states sweeping your reality are to help you find more ways to shine.

You want to be happy? Of course you do, no one says, 'I want to be born, so I can live a life of suffering and die miserably and miserable.' You want lives of satisfaction and accomplishment, challenge and joy.

You wonder that if you are really the creator and are truly as clever as we have been telling you…then why are you not happy?

So you read your lists, your books, and do everything you can find to clear yourself. You look at your rooms, you call the moving van to take that which you do not need away, and you still are not happy. Where, you ask, is your happiness?

And you, as children, scream up to the heavens, 'I want to be happy! When will you give me happiness?!' As if your happiness could be created by anyone other than yourself, as if anyone else truly had that much power over you, as if your soul would ever surrender that much of your sovereignty to anyone else. As long as you look at happiness as something that you can be made to feel, you will fail.

It is not that wanting to be happy is at fault here, or is unattainable. It is that you have made it a goal.

Happiness is not a goal, it is a road. It's not a destination, it's a path. Do you understand the difference in this? It is not a separate state that can be brought to you; it is a manner of being, of perceiving yourself in relationship to the rest of the universe.

You say, 'I will strive all of my life and build these bridges and climb these mountains and swim all of those awful rivers and walk across the hot, burning sands of the deserts, and be almost drowned in the deluge. I will put off my feelings and my heart and all that I would enjoy doing, because I don't want to waste time, I want to reach 'happy' as quickly as possible. I want to get to 'happy' where I can finally relax and enjoy my life.'

And you wonder and sulk why you have not – finally – reached your happiness.

'Happy' is the road you take. It is the steps you make. It is the joy in accomplishment in climbing those mountains, the pleasure in meeting with other people and finding a way to build that bridge together. It is loving the feel of the rain on your bodies and looking across the deserts and saying, 'Isn't this grand, and I am strong enough to make it, and I will glory in my strength.'

That is happy – looking at the path that you have placed in front of you, every step, all of it, and finding joy in every step.

Happiness is a process. It is not a goal, it's not a place, it's not a destination. It's the process of your life.

So then, how to be happy? Do what you like, if you do not like what you are doing, do something different, or do it differently. If you do not like what you do, it is a sign that you are not doing the right thing. Find what you like, find your passion.

But what if you don't know what you like, you don't know what is in your own heart. Dear ones, if you don't know who you are, how can you possibly find out what you want to do with who you are.

And so that's what all of these energy waves are to help you to do. To find out who you are, to help you understand the workings of your human heart. This is the doorway to happiness – self-knowledge, understanding your heart – and trusting that the universe will bring you that which will make your heart happy…once you find a way to discover all of the little doorways and the rooms and the cellars and the attics that are hidden within your heart.

Think back on your life, and think of it as a path that you have taken from the start to this moment in your time. Think of all the places you have walked and the people you have walked with, think of all you have done and the stops you have made and all of the experience you have collected like snapshots in an album.

Part of the process that you are all being asked to go through, is to look backward upon your path and find those things that you were not able to embrace into your being. Find those things that caused you so much hardship, such emotional stress that you took a little part of your heart - the part that hurt so desperately - and you put it in a dark room and you closed the door, and said, 'I will not think of this again. It hurts too much.'

You felt anger at that which you wanted but could not get, so you put that in another little room, and put a bar across it. 'I do not want to feel my anger, it makes me less of a person, I will not confront that.' And you walked away from it.

You experienced fears in your lives, and they made you feel inept and out of control. So you put them in a big, vast room, and there you bricked up the front of it, 'I will not look at these fears, because the fears lead me to believe I'm not in control, and I will be swallowed up whole by that which I do not understand.'

And so you have built this great mansion inside yourself filled with rooms and closets and attics and basements, each containing pieces and parts of yourself because that's what your experiences are you. They are your life, they are expressions and manifestations of your being, of your soul, your mastery, your sovereignty.

Look at all those parts of yourself, even those awful, wretched little things that give you such displeasure, 'How could I have done that? That was an awful thing I did, I am so ashamed.'

You all have within you things of which you are deeply ashamed, because you have judged yourself as being unworthy. The dark parts of yourself you put behind doors and you brick them up - these are the ones that the energy at this time is butting up against like rams against great boulders.

And you wonder why you shake, you wonder why your reality shakes. Your earth mirrors what is going on within all of you...she is accommodating that way. What you are unable to get on an energy level, she will manifest for you in your third dimension, so that you will face it.

You are creating situations in front of you that mirror those that are behind all those doorways, all those locks and bars and bricks.

Unless you find a way to open those doors and take those bricks and that mortar down, these things will lurk there all of your lives and come out when you least expect it and least appreciate it...all fangs and teeth. They will take control of your life and trip you up.

It is not us doing this to you, it is yourself. It is these parts of yourself you have not faced with courage and with forgiveness and embraced into your being.

You must look at the most awful things you have ever done and been, and say, 'I love you regardless, you represent where I chose to walk to reach enlightenment and I love you and I forgive you.' Open the doors and let the light in so you may shine more brightly.

Life is not a cruel play, and you the unknowing, unthinking actors, that we, with all our strings, jerk around. You are the masters who chose to come here to do all of this.

You need to understand that you do this as a grand service for your world. For you are each processing issues for many others on your planet, you are here because each of you in some manner recognize the seed of the light within you, and you know that when it begins to unfold it will become a loving umbrella of healing energies that comfort those around you, that protect your planet.

So when you face your worst, darkest little rooms, trust that you are not doing it alone, nor for your own single purpose. You are doing it with the full love of the universe behind you, for we help you in every way that is fitting and that you allow us to.

You do it for the purpose of saving your world. You do it for the purpose of increasing the understanding of all of your reality.

You do it for love. You do it for love of each other, for yourselves, and for the acknowledgment that somewhere within you is the God that you are.

Look not in judgment on any part of you, or on anything you have done. Look not in fear or despair on anything you have chosen to experience in your lives. Think not that you are lesser and that another is greater.

If you were puny, fearsome little people, you would not be here to be awakened. You would simply shut the door harder in your little, cluttered rooms and read comic books, as children. This is all you would do, and you would live out the rest of your lives in blissful deaf, dumb, blind ignorance. And you'd think that's all there would be.

But you have chosen to wake up, and is it not a shock to illuminate those awful, dark rooms in which you have spent all of your lives cowering in fear and ignorance. It is hard once you begin to wake up not to look at those parts in judgment and say, 'Now I am so spiritually evolved, but wasn't I terrible, wasn't I unforgivable, before?'

You would not judge a child for its inability to walk when it could not.

A child crawls, and then, stumbling, pulls itself up and falls down and falls down again and again, and takes another brave step and falls down yet again. We are the loving parents who applaud each step, who try to put the little pillows under your little bottoms so you would not fall quite so hard.

Do not look in judgment upon those stumbling little steps you made earlier in your development, look at all that you have done in love, in acceptance, in forgiveness. Love yourselves. How could you not love yourself? You are God. How could you not look at another and love every part of them? They are God.

That is why you are here, to transcend the judgments of separation, to transcend the judgments of fear, pain, anger, to transcend the judgments of that awful, little room you spent all of your lives constructing.

'Why could I have not gotten it earlier?" you say. Well, you got it when you got it. Do not be in judgment, be in acceptance.

Look at your lives, reassess the paths you have chosen to take - not in terms of measuring their effectiveness...did they get you to that magical place called happy? But look on them and ask each step how it prepared you to find who you are.

Can you not look at each step and see the joy in each step as you would look upon a child, stumbling, trying to maintain its balance. Look upon yourselves with love. Why not? This is what life is.

Once you learn how to do that, once you become in harmony with your soul – the Godself – within you, then that which you manifest in your world will become filled with joy, and will no longer be those little dark rooms with locks and keys and bricks and mortar that you need in order to keep yourself safe from those demons within you.

Be in joy. Life is not a torment, it is not suffering, it is not a punishment. It is a game – a game. And know that when you get good enough at this, you can change the rules and play another game.

Above all, do not let someone on the sidelines look at what you are doing and tell you how incompetent you are. Do not join them in condemnation of your efforts. Accept every step you take for the purpose that you made it – the purpose of self-knowledge. Do not allow someone else to look at you and say you did poorly. That is not acceptable, to assign your feelings of self-worth to another.

Do you know the goal of life? It is not to reach what you call happiness; it is to reach the ability to love all that is around you and within you without condition. That is the purpose of life and that is what truly is happiness.

Once you attain that, then you can play any game you wish, as many as you wish, wherever you wish, in whatever form you wish, for that is your pleasure, and that is your capability.

Do you understand this?

Know that when someone says, 'These are the rules, follow them or suffer the punishment.' Look at them, smile, walk away and play your game your own way. You do not have to be a missionary and convince them of your truth That is their truth – God help them, their truth; and if that is their truth, that is what they must live with.

Choose a reality that will bring you joy. Let go of all judgment, particularly of yourself. It is considered sophisticated to look upon yourself and say, 'I am such a fool, if I had only not done that.'

You think that you are somehow buying people's acceptance when you make fun of yourself, but you are not. What you are doing is judging some part of yourself as being outside of the light, and if you believe that, it is so. Do not look harshly upon yourself.

We are not here to tell you how to run your lives and we are not here to tell you that this is serving and that is not, that you should all quit your jobs and run off into the woods and pick herbs and wear bark.

We are here to tell you that whatever you choose in your lives, choose it with your heart, and if you cannot choose it with your heart, then choose something you can. Please think on this for a moment. Pause here and reread this paragraph. It is of vast importance in your life.

If you do not know your heart, how do you expect life to bring you joy.

Make your lives an outpicturing of what you feel and who you are. There is joy in everything you do, or can be if you learn how to look at it properly, if you look at it not in judgment, but look at it as something you have chosen to experience to learn something of yourself.

Life is not filled with a series of painful, arduous classrooms, 'Isn't this awful, but I will have to get through this, for I've signed up for it and I must do this.' It is not that at all, and you will not buy a better 'grade' by taking wretched courses. Life is not about suffering…it does not even have to be irritating.

You do not have to buy your salvation with pain and denial of self; that is a convenient belief that was created in order to control you in your history by all those who had much to gain by owning your power, by denying your sovereignty, by keeping you a victim. Understand you this?

You were told that if you were good little boys and girls and did not raise a fuss as your power was being taken from you, when you were forced in little boxes, little behaviors, little feelings, little beliefs...that if you were good, you would then go to heaven with the angels and strum harps all the time.

What your life is, is what your life is. And, every moment of your life is your heaven.

Heaven is not a place to go, it is that road you are on.

Happiness is not a destination, why put it off? Anything that you make a destination, you have put outside of yourself. Why would you do such a thing? Why would you say, 'If I'm good enough, I will find happiness.' Why separate it from you?

Put your happiness within your reality now by agreeing that it is each step you take, and then find joy in every step you take.

Say to yourself, 'I have chosen this experience to learn certain skills, so that I will have a vaster capacity for joy as I walk. I will become stronger, I will become more mighty, I will become greater, and this is why I have chosen these things.'

Is this becoming somewhat irritating...this endless repetition on the nature of happiness and choice? Deal with it. You have been programmed throughout your life to think a certain way, to believe there are victims and perpetrators and goals and that the ends justify the means and no pain no gain. Do you really think one sentence – even an incredibly brilliant one – will erase all that negative programming?

You have to focus your attention on overcoming your old thought-forms in order to create a new set of more effective ideas with which to run your life.

You have to revisit the past in order to heal it, you have to embrace all your choices in order to learn from them; and then you must let go of the results of the unserving choices in order to make room for all that is more serving.

So, look back on all of those steps of your lives that caused you such blisters - the ones that felt as though you were walking on burning coals and broken glass. Look back on those in kindness and forgiveness. Know that you chose those experiences to teach you something important.

It might have been to open your compassionate heart.

You, who have known what pain feels like, will empathize when someone comes to you in pain and asks for solace. You are able to fully open your compassionate heart and understand what they have gone through, for you share that experience; and you will know what healing they need, for you have required it yourself.

You have labored long. It is to make you strong, it is to have given you the tools to make your road of happiness a rich, full one, one in which you can come into your mastery, one in which you can then turn to others around you and know what they need to heal and grow. And, in that giving and accepting, there is such joy that each step on your road will vibrate within you with pure pleasure.

Your lives are not silly, nor wasted, nor puny; your lives are full of experiences, of things you have put in front of you in order to learn something and to become stronger.

Love yourselves for that, love yourselves for every step. We do, we love you greatly. You are those who have chosen to come here at great cost, to be here in great challenge, and then in great joy, and to be of service for those who are not as clever as you are.

Even without your actively working to help another, your energy is processing the grief and the pain and the fears for others who have not gotten as far as you have, for those who are too afraid to shine the light in their cluttered little rooms...because they are afraid of what they will see once they do such a thing.

You have chosen to be incarnate here and now, to be the beacons of light for those who are not quite strong enough to do it for themselves. Be a flashlight, be a great torch. Be a lighthouse in your reality, let your light shine forth wherever you go.

You do not have to speak in words, you have to simply look at another and open your heart to them and they will feel it. They will. You have felt such things yourselves when you meet certain people and stand next to them and feel warmed. On some level, you knew you were standing next to those who have chosen to be light, and you are warmed by the grace of their love and of the acceptance of their soul.

You have all chosen to do this, as well, for others. So go forth, dear ones, and do this.

This is your happiness.

{ 10 }

Feel what you feel

SO...NOW YOU'RE AWARE OF THE ENERGY WAVES sweeping across your reality in order to stir up all those deep, hard-to-reach things inside of you, those things you least want to face.

Sometimes these waves will be so intense, they could easily manifest physiological effects in your bodies. You might have some temperature shifting within your bodies, waves of warmth, for example. Some of you might even feel a bit lightheaded at times, or with a headache. You might even have moments of blurring in your vision. These symptoms are brief, however. Do not let them concern you...unless of course, they continue for days. That could certainly be a sign of a much deeper manifestation from different causes and you should treat such possibilities accordingly.

But we are talking about the physical effects created by this time of great energetic stimulation. If you understand how simply to ride these energy waves, the effects will be transitory and mild.

The intent of these waves is to create some very distinctive reprogramming within your individual energy fields. They are here to help in your awakening, in your evolution as a master. This is part of your agreement at this time and it can be as easy or as difficult as you choose to make it. An understanding of this will make it far easier.

For a moment, imagine you are in the ocean in your own little boat. Now imagine that the sea is getting increasingly rough. The waves are beginning to come higher and higher, and you are afraid that you will be swept and swamped by the waves and the currents.

You cling tightly to an anchor line that is fastened to the sea floor beneath the water. Imagine this. The line, your 'safety' line, cannot get longer. Imagine.

Feel yourself hanging on for dear life. Now...feel the waves continue to get higher. However, your line does not get longer, so the waves begin to break over you. You're afraid to let go of the anchor, you can hardly breathe for all the water. Feel your terror.

Now, understand that if you insist on hanging onto this little line in your little boat, thinking it will save you, it will not. If you would but let go, you could find your self buoyed up by the waves.

Allow this metaphor to sink in on a deep level. This is an important one. This will help you to ride the waves; this will help you to keep your head and not be swamped by these vast currents of energy that are sweeping across your reality.

The more you hold on to these rigid, little lines that you think will save you out of fear, the more the waves will crash over your head and slowly drown you.

Know that in your reality these will become greater and greater. Over the next few years, some of the waves will become quite intense. You have all experienced them. Some of them have outpictured in your planet, some of them have outpictured in your population, some of them in your individual realities – all as great, surging upheavals.

Understand the power of letting go. Whatever you think you must hang onto in order to save you, are old pictures of outmoded beliefs and perceptions and actions. Accept that you have chosen this moment to see that the line you are holding onto has outlived its usefulness and is no longer adequate for your life.

So let go, allow yourself to be buoyed up; you may be swept to a new and far more exciting place.

Of course, the other option, when you are heading into the unknown, and hence into greater risk, is to ensure you are well prepared. Check the forecast. Bring a longer anchor line. Pay attention to the weather. Pack a life jacket. Pick a bigger boat. You get the idea.

Trust is important. So is preparation. This book is about both, on some level the same thing.

Now accept that this is happening according to your agreements and with your accord. You have ordered this. The energies coming down in your reality are for the purpose of delivering to you, giving you the tools – the energy – to create what you desire in your life...for your highest good.

Why are we beating you up with these waves of energy? Because there is much to be accomplished and time is running out. We're giving you a series of time compressions so your time can be much more effective, so you can accomplish far more in the next few years.

What do you need to accomplish? Do you know? Do you know why you're here, what you're looking for, what you're supposed to keep, or release? What if you make the wrong choice, will that make you miss your chance to move on and doom you to yet another round in this reality? Does the fear of that make you immobile, uncertain, afraid to make any choice for fear they are the wrong ones?

Let us help you through these great quandaries.

Let's start with why you are here. By experiencing all the rich options of third-dimensional existence, you create a greater understanding of life; and by adding more and more experience in your life, you serve to raise the vibration - the awareness - of all.

There are two issues we will talk about here. One, the issue of how do you know the answers to any of those questions, even if you stumble upon them. The second issue is...what you know, all will know. What moves within one, moves within all. Let that sink in a moment. That is a big truth to absorb.

But let us start with one, single individual...what moves within one. How do you know what you want. How do you know what you are here for. How do you know what you are not here for. How do you know what you are to change, to seek out, to alter, to refine....to let go, to leave behind, to run from as quickly as you can.

One way you know is to listen for messengers. They come with gifts of insight and clarity. Sometimes loud and unmistakable, sometimes quiet and mysterious; sometimes the messengers are as subtle as opening a book and noticing a passage with strangely pertinent text. At times we might blow a gust of wind in such a way to make you look in a certain direction and see something that imprints on your awareness, or causes you to turn on the TV at the right moment, or turn a corner and run into a friend, or drop a pile of papers and something, something in the way they fall evokes a thought.

The short answer is that everything in your reality brings you information.

The long answer is that everything in your reality is designed to trigger an internal process that will guide you to the part of yourself that already knows what you seek.

The truest answer is that your soul calls for clues (which we oblige by creating) in your environment to trigger your physical being to send you your own messengers. Do you know what they are, these messengers of awareness, of knowledge? Can you not guess?

Correct! They are your feelings, your emotional states.

What you feel is your own soul telling you what you need or don't need, what you want or don't want, what you should and should not do...what is to your detriment and what is for your highest good.

You have everything you need in your own selves to know what you should do. You just don't believe in that ability, in fact, you've been taught to dismiss it.

This is not an abstraction, this is not simply a philosophy; this is a blueprint for your existence.

Those who programmed your bodies, who designed the fundamental building blocks of your physicality, were very clever with your DNA. Even with all those strands disconnected, it works exceedingly well.

How do you work as an organism? You are a collection of cells, but what keeps the cells together; what tells them what to do, how to behave, and when to act? What gives your physical being the animation and purpose to work?

It starts with intention, you might say sacred or divine intention: thought that has contemplated itself and is self aware, a part of the infinite God wanting to know itself through experience and expand the potential of All That Is.

This divine intention organizes energy into matter, according to the rules of the dimension in which it chooses to experience reality – rules that govern gross behavior of the matter within that dimension (though intention can certainly bend and break the rules of that dimensional arena if desired and agreed-upon by the participants...but that is a complex topic that would digress us far outside of what we wish to discuss here).

The manner that divine intention communicates to its physical manifestations in this reality is through electro-magnetic energy, a form of light. All matter in this universe shares this field, the field that helps animate our beingness.

Animals can read it. Plants can read it. Even rocks. You can, too. Your minds however have become so focused on your physical senses, as we have said, that it has become much like a whisper hiding in a bowling alley.

The biological component of this field is simple. Sadly, it is something that the mind not only has trouble hearing because of its dependence on physical experience, but has been trained not to trust even if does hear it.

It is emotion. Your emotional states are your own messengers, to tell you truths your rational mind cannot possibly know.

How does it work? Each cell in your body is covered with tiny receptors. Your spirit – your unlimited mind – tells your cells what to do through chemical messengers called neural peptides. They bring emotional states to your cells, which accept direction regarding what they are to do next – more attention here, less attention there.

This is how you were constructed, how your bodies were built to translate intention into experience.

Your bodies were designed to give you all you need to know about how to create and refine your lives. The fundamental dynamic of your physiology gives you all the clues you need to understand what is important to you at any particular moment in your time.

You add all of these messages together, and they create states of feeling within you that direct your attention, your action, your choices.

If you close yourself off from the macro-emotion of all of the dynamics going on within you on a chemical, physical, micro-minute level, you are closing yourself off from existence and negating the fundamentals of your bodies and their design.

There is also a danger, a physiological danger of shutting yourself off from your emotional states. Do you really think your soul will let your personality off the hook if there is something you need to get in order to proceed in your development? Think about this. They will simply turn the volume up until you do get it.

Your soul sends out neural peptides to carry messages to your cells, your physical body. You ignore them? 'I will not look at fear, it diminishes me, I look not at anger, it threatens me. I will not look at pain, it is too frightening.'

Do you really think your soul will give up? You turn the volume up. If you will not look at it, you turn the volume higher.

And you still do not look at it? All of these messengers running around and no one listening to them? Where do you think disease comes from, where do you think the energy state that invites accident comes from. Worse, where do you think depression comes from – depression is the state of not feeling. You become so overloaded that you don't let yourself feel anything; you are deaf, dumb and blind and there is no worse curse in existence.

So, do you know how to move along your path of evolution? Do not be afraid to look at anything you feel, do not denigrate your emotions, do not say 'This is not worthy of a spiritual being.'

What do you think spirit is?

Spirit is not sitting around humming 'Ommm.' It is not sitting on a great mountaintop contemplating colors. Spirit is that which has manifested all in this reality. All. To be true to your spiritual nature means to get out into your world and connect with your part in it, it is finding the connections within you.

What tells you of these connections are your emotional states, these are integral to your existence, to your evolution. If you do not let yourself feel what you feel, you might as well be dead; for you will be soon. And you will die flat, without feeling, having wasted this chance and all the opportunities of this rich life, in this glorious place you have chosen. There is no emotion that is so awful that you should believe, 'I cannot feel such a thing, it is too terrifying.'

Embrace it, love it, embrace the feelings that are given to you by your soul to get your attention and ask them what you are to learn from them.

This is why you are here. To enjoy the treasures and the pleasures of this life. This is how you clear yourself, to help yourself come to awareness, to joy. You look at all these emotional states; they are here to help you enjoy life. Know there is nothing within you that is not beautiful, that is not glorious, that is not perfect in our eyes.

Love yourself, love all of your emotional states, love your flesh and be with yourself. Once you love yourself, you can then turn to others and they will sense within you this infinite light of love, of acceptance, of power, and they will both respond to you and be transformed by you.

That is how you access your power, that is how you turn your own volume up. That is how you teach others...by example, by living your spiritual reality.

Because you are not simply individuals on this planet. That which moves so freely within each one of you affects those around you. You use your feelings to love yourself, and then you become a beacon of wholeness.

What moves within you, moves within everyone. This is your gift to your reality. You are not separate from him, nor her, nor any one of you, nor I. We are all One, we are simply different faces of the One.

What moves within you, moves within all. What you feel, another will benefit. What makes you grow, helps them, because you are not little islands bound by flesh. You are flesh that is the manifestation of the feeling which is the energy of God expressed in reality.

There are no boundaries. That which you feel does not stop at your skin. As we have said, your universe does not start outside your body; your universe is seamless and you are part of the very fabric.

What you feel will affect the person next to you and the person next to that. That which you will not look at becomes deaf and blind for another. What you allow yourself to embrace, in strength and in courage, helps someone else embrace it, too.

What moves in one, moves in all. For these rich messengers that move within you, move beyond you to others, and their receptors feel your messengers. They feel you.

When you stand next to one and you like or do not like them, it's because you are responding in a literally non-rational manner toward them. You stand next to someone and you feel something of what they feel, you do not know it consciously and you do not trust it if you do feel it. Nevertheless, you are in communication with them

Someone walks into a room and the room brightens, the energies of everyone in the room heighten. The awareness lifts, the room is somehow more vivid, more colorful.

And, there are people who come into a room and everyone droops. The energy levels ebb, people feel a bit closed off, somewhat depressed. The person may be sad, or totally self-absorbed; they add nothing to the room, or they take all the energy and hoard it, like greedy children.

You can help even them. Simply imagine you are giving that poor, sad, tired, deaf, dumb, selfish person a beam of light from your heart. Give it in love, not in judgment, not in pity, but in love - simply because they are another face of you.

They will brighten, if they can. Of course, also understand there are times when one has chosen to be in such a difficult state. They are waiting to gain the strength to listen to their own messengers. But there is no one who is so closed off who cannot benefit from the light that each one of you is capable of beaming.

You who can change the world and heal a continent, and you shall. You who can help children everywhere, and you shall. You who know how to make people laugh and heal and expand, and you shall. You can do it all.

Understand why you are here – to feel. This is not an abstract philosophy. It is a tangible, practical way to live in health and wholeness.

If a belief in science helps you to believe this, fine; then go get a textbook, read about your bodies, and think about how clever those were who designed the reality in which they could be created, how they designed the fact that emotion is stored in the body. And then learn how you can transmute and release unprocessed emotions and how you can help others do the same.

Learn to reveal the light that comprises each one of you. Allow the grayness to fall off, the grayness that comes from the lack of awareness of what you feel, from the fears of what you feel, 'If I feel these things, I will be swamped. If I feel these dreadful emotions, I will not be the good, little boy or girl I was raised to be. If I feel my anger, they will not love me, they will punish me. If I express my fear, they will take advantage of me, they will use me, judge me. If I show my pain, the people will run from me, as though I were an infected virus.'

Feel all of it, let all you feel sweep through you. Some of it does not feel healthy, it does not feel good at all – there is some understatement in this. Some of it is wretched, and some of it will be worse. For this we are sad, but not sorry. Some things must be.

You who have allowed yourselves through too many existences to have forgotten the Godself within, that you are sacred, that you are beautiful, that you are without limits...you've forgotten this as you've forgotten all of those lives you have enjoyed. You've forgotten who you are, and you've layered yourselves over with so much.

Don't you wish sometimes you had invisible cloaks you could wrap around your bodies and disappear within so that the world would not notice you, so they would put their arrows away and you would no longer be such an easy target.

Stand there and take it. Know that you can access all the energy you will ever need to heal, and know that every place you find a wound is a place where you can heal yourself and allow more light to shine through.

There is so much you have held onto for so long out of ignorance, out of forgetfulness. You think your lives hurt, you think there is no justice, you think there is no happy ending. You think that what is, will always be. There will be unfairness, there will be victims, there will be loss and grief and terror; there will be pain and suffering, and there will be people starving and people angry and people who torture and murder.

All of these things are symptoms of those who have forgotten how to feel.

Once you embrace your feeling, you find that you are not the individual island of consciousness, you are not alone, you are part of All That Is. And if you allow yourself to feel – truly feel – deep down into the deepest, hardest parts of yourself, you would find staring back from that bottomless well, the God looking back at you saying, 'I love you and you are not alone.'

You are never alone.

It is only in your experience and your pain and anger and fears that you think you are, and so it hurts worse. So you say, 'I do not wish to feel this.' You put the cloak on and try to push these things away.

Why do you think we turn the volume up? If you do not pay attention, it goes up again, and up again, and up again.

You are so clever, so gifted, you've gotten very, very good at hiding from what you felt had hurt so much; you judged it and you would not let yourself feel it.

Through lifetimes and lifetimes of unresolved, unblended feeling, you burdened yourself with what you think of as 'karmic debt.' It does not signify what you believe. Your burdens are simply layers that you have carried with you of experience from past lifetimes that you did not assimilate into your awareness because you judged them negative, painful, horrific. Then, you stuffed them someplace deep and dark so you would not have to deal with them.

Karma is not an unyielding concrete cloak that you must put on. All you have to do is to feel in order to let go of even that.

These waves of energy in your reality are to help find those parts of yourself that you hid away because you didn't want to feel them.

With these waves, there will be much emotion that will be brought up, there might be memories attached that make no sense to you. Don't even try. The awareness will not come from your mind on these. Your mind could be driven mad by your attempt to impose the yardsticks of your present reality on these things you will be forced to feel. Simply be with them, allow them to wash over you and off you, and then you will not have to carry them any longer.

What will be underneath all of this? Joy. Power. Creativity. Belonging. Awareness. Compassion. Energy. All you ever wanted.

Greater still? Community. Within all of you is the doorway to the perfect sacred communion of each of you to everyone who shares this universe with you.

What else is the purpose of life other than to feel this love?

{ 11 }

Karmic agreements and other children's stories

IF YOU HAVE BEEN TRULY ABSORBING THIS, you are likely starting to notice some deep and unsettling symptoms – physical, emotional, situational.

We've mentioned some of the physical ones – headaches, warmth, lightheadedness. What about your dreams? What about the relationships in your life, your work? Has your boss been a bit different, your friends, family?

Things you thought were smooth and contained all of a sudden jumped up and began demanding your attention. People you thought you knew have begun to react oddly around you, more needy, more contentious.

Are you finding you are irritated by things you used to enjoy, people you used to enjoy?

Is your life beginning to feel unfamiliar, out of control?

It's for a purpose. Trust in this. That is, of course, the ultimate lesson of all of this, to get you all to find the courage to be in trust.

And in truth, less trusting in spirit...it is really about trusting in yourself.

Isn't that a hard thing to develop in your reality. When all of your lives and all of your teachers, your parents, friends, the media, your leaders and gurus have all taken trust from you. This is a hard one, is it not?

Those of you who choose to get through all this information - this reprogramming – you should be applauded; you are paying attention. You have noticed something strange and wonderful out there that has your name on it, so to speak.

You have agreed to hear this. I am not talking about conscious agreement, not the ego self, not the puny limited mind you have burdened yourselves with so far, but the grand Godself within each one of you. It is you, that part of you that chose to put your bodies here and absorb all this, so that you would get an acceleration in your evolution.

It is as though you are on a grand, cosmic roller coaster. You will go up and down and around and around. You will feel like you will crash, but if you pay any attention at all, you know how a roller coaster works – great bars come down and hold you in place. So all you have to learn to do is sit back, enjoy the ride and trust that it will not let you crash.

The difference here is that you are the one who designed where it is taking you, where it will travel with all of its heights and dips and loops. This is by your agreement, you came here to do this.

When you decided to pick up this book and consider all these ideas, it's because you wanted a jump start on your path.

You've been going around and around – it was getting boring doing the same loops, over and over again. You were getting nowhere and you were bored and you couldn't find your power. You were stuck in the same little cars, with the same little people, and after a while...it lost its charm.

So, you come to us and we tune the engine up a peg and pull the lever and off you go in a new direction, faster, higher, grander.

You don't have to buckle down, clench your fists and cling to the bar with all your strength...just be in trust. You might have some physical symptoms as a result of this; your body temperatures might rise at times, you might have trouble sleeping. As we have said, they will be transitory. They are simply the physical manifestations of the huge changes that are taking place within you...changes that you asked for.

You must believe that none of this is being done to you. You are not victims, you are co-creators in all of this; you are the ones asking for an intensification, an acceleration of your path to mastery. You make a choice to go faster and we oblige.

We could tell you to enjoy it, but we know that you are unlikely to release your fears as easily as that. It is not that you are necessarily dependent on your limitation, it is that you are used to it. And human nature is such that you are comfortable with what you're used to...it is difficult at times to shake you loose from your comfort zones.

If you find it too alien to enjoy the loss of control in your life, we then ask that you simply relax somewhat as this roller coaster gains speed. You'll have great fun, careening around crazy corners, turning upside down; you'll swoop up to dizzying heights and roar into desperate depths...and best off all, you'll reach all sorts of exciting new places. You'll learn to love the adventure. As you get closer and closer to your mastery, to your Godself, you will become increasingly impatient with the old, the familiar.

How courageous this is, for we know what is out there, outside of your safe little tracks, is the unknown. We know how frightening that is, how much it kicks up all of your fears. It is hard to be in trust when you are frightened of the unknown.

If you think we're going to scold you for being frightened, you're wrong. We're going to tell you that we love you for the courage it took to come here and ask us to kick you into the fast lane. It is hard. It is easier to stay in your safe little lives that go nowhere. But then, what fun is that? This is not why you came here.

There is a wise woman in your reality who once said, 'A ship in harbor is safe, but that is not what ships are built for.'

You came into your lives, in this now, to head out with your ships and explore vast continents of possibilities. To test the boundaries of reality, to see what rules can be broken and stretch truths to the limit. To expand the consciousness of All. To make a difference. You did not want to stay stuck in the safe and the sane.

We know it's hard, and so we commend you, we applaud you and we love you for your courage. It's hard to step off the cliff, is it not? But what a grand ride when you have learned how to fly. And this is what you have all chosen to do, to step off your cliff into the unknown.

Know we will not let you fall. You will either learn to flap your wings very well or we will catch you and support you until you can.

So you have begun. Wonderful. You will start feeling the manifestations of your choices, some of you already are. You might feel a bit 'twitchy.' This is to be expected, you are changing the very nature of who and what you are.

Here is a good exercise to keep your physicality somewhat grounded: Put your feet on the floor and imagine that in the middle of your room is a great golden light. Call it the Christ light, the God light, the infinite light of Spirit, whatever resonates with your being. Breathe it in and send it down through the bottom of your feet into the body of the earth. That will help ground you through times of great inner change.

If you feel in need of even more intense grounding, immerse yourself in a bath, or, far more satisfying – and one of the great gifts in your reality – embrace another...that is an exceptionally effective form of grounding. You should be smiling right now.

Does this surprise you, that I have such a regard for the physical expression of your beingness? Why should I not? I have experienced the richness of your existence as well, and developed great passion for the humanness of you.

There are uncountable legions of us who have spent lives on this wondrous planet and then chose to come back in service, for we understand what you have signed up for. We understand the pleasure of it all, and the challenge, the sorrows, the winning, the not winning, the pain and the joy.

We understand what your bodies bring to you in knowledge and in pleasure and in grief...they are rich companions. They bring you much and they enhance greatly your experience and your awareness of the glory of life. Love them.

Your bodies are not the second-rate citizens, your spirits the exalted. Not at all. If your bodies were not important, then why would you have chosen to be here. Enjoy your bodies, honor them, respect them as you would your spirit. You are both and each nourishes and supports the other. Enjoy each as equals, each in a delicious dance of life on this remarkable planet.

Do not abuse them or neglect them. Take them out for a walk, allow them the pleasure of interacting with your beautiful planet and its extraordinary sensations. You would do that for a pet, why not your bodies.

And, do not give them away lightly. This is important.

There are many sorrowful things on your planet now that are largely for the purpose of teaching you not to give your bodies away lightly. And there are many brave souls who have chosen to participate in these painful events in order to be the teachers of this. To show you the cost if you give your bodies away casually to those in whom you have not developed trust. To those with whom you have no history, no commitment, who have no kinship, no ties.

Understand that some lessons are cloaked in beauty and radiance, to show you where you need to go, to give you incentive to seek the positive. Some lessons, however, are the opposite – lessons wrapped in rags and decay, in pain and remorse. These are the warning signs, as though they are great cosmic lighthouses, telling you to come no closer, for here be rocks that will dash your future.

These sad and destructive events in your reality, that show you the consequences of intimacy without trust, are your lighthouses, your great warning beacons.

Your bodies are sovereign creations of your sacred spirit. Treat them with respect. Love your bodies, honor them. That is the lesson.

So, as you are learning to love yourself – all aspects of yourself – which is the real purpose of all of this, and the only true road to mastery, we will be creating all sorts of lessons to help you find that sacred state.

At this time, you are apt to find your bodies stirred up, stimulated...itchy. You might be feeling a slight tingling in the palms of your hands at this moment, or a slight warmth in your heart area. These are all signs that you are experiencing expansion of your being. As you continue to clear yourself, as you evolve and your spirit expands, your bodies can't help but feel the results of that.

We know you've already cleared a lot and you're tired of it; but just think of it as another great run on your roller coaster. Love the process, dear ones, you will be doing this for many, many years.

You have already spent much time clearing your bodies, your light bodies and physical bodies, of old thought patterns, old emotions, old unprocessed events, old fears, sorrows and angers...all the unnecessary stuff you have accumulated through this life. You have dealt with your careers, your relationships, with your parents, friends, enemies.

You have faced obsolete belief structures, trying to go from the small, limited mind and belief system to a larger one that will encompass those things that cannot be measured by your senses and your scientific methodologies.

You have on some level dealt, or at least have started to deal, with all of these. Kicking up quite a fuss, are they not. You are unhappy in your jobs, you are unhappy in many of your relationships. You are all too often unhappy in your lives.

Excellent. It shows you are paying attention, you are noticing the things that no longer serve you.

Good start. But did you wonder if there are underlying causes for all these unserving things, that maybe these are just echoes, or mirrors, of issues and events from a much older time that need to be cleared - issues and events not of this life? That which is termed 'karma'?

Ahh...the 'big' one. Karma, the lesson you cannot see, the one that you never know is coming, the bullet with your name on it.

How do you prepare for something you know nothing about. You can't. Knowledge is not the issue, trust is the issue.

You choose your lives – all of them – like actors choose roles to learn something, to experience something that seems interesting to you. But because there have been events in your lives that were so emotionally intense, you did not resolve them. So, you stored this unresolved emotion on your etheric body like a pocket of tar.

Then that life comes to an end, and all of these things that were not resolved you carried forth with you on your etheric body – the garment of your soul as it were. Then another life. So you create some events that mirror those old pockets of unresolved emotion that you had stored on yourself. If you resolve these, they open to the light, you are lighter and you go on. If you still do not resolve – or master - those issues, the pocket becomes larger and the events in the next life, and the next, become larger as well.

This happens over all of your lives. You create, you process, you create, you process...but you keep building more and more and more that you have not been able to deal with. Understand you this?

Now, this is the life that you have chosen to bring all of those great, unresolved issues to deal with. You chose.

You chose.

The karmic wheel, as it is sometimes called, is a children's story. You somehow feel that a nasty God has inspected your life and said, 'You did not do that one well, so you are going to have to pay for that in the next life. We will write this one up.' And this angry deity follows you around with this cosmic report card, 'C, all right. D, tsk, tsk - you really should do that one again. F... oh that was so awful you have to pay for your failure. An A, all right!, good job!...we'll release you from some other stuff then.'

Not so.

Life and all of its variety and variables is not something that is done to you, it is something that you choose. You choose your lives to learn what you wish. If you do not learn them well, you say, 'I still want to learn them.' So you carry them with you into another life to do so.

You choose to take the class over again. Pay attention to this. If you get this, you will understand that if you get what you are placing in front of you, you can close the class down.

If you get it, you can stop it.

Karma is about restoring balance to your soul. It is your choice, you are not the victims. If there are patterns in your life, over and over and over again, each time getting bigger and bigger and bigger, know it is probably connected to a karmic agreement. It is an old event that you have brought with you into this life and you have agreed to deal with it at all costs. I would suggest you find a way to do so.

Search out your patterns, go into the stillness of your being, go backward; try to imagine where the original pattern came from. Feel the emotion that may not have anything to do with that which is in front of you, but has leapt up and grabbed you by the throat and caused you to raise a great hue and cry.

Have you ever found yourselves all of a sudden reacting completely out of proportion to some event that is in front of you? So violently that you think you are going mad? It is because you are reacting to some stored pocket of unresolved emotion that you have been carrying with you for so very many lives.

But this is the one where you've chosen to open it and release the toxic contents...because this is when you've given yourself no other reasonable choice. This is the life in which your reality will change so significantly that unless you get these core issues, you will not be invited to play in the next level for another millennium.

Your reality is ascending to a higher level, a higher vibration. This does not mean if you don't get it you will be forever stuck in purgatory; it does not mean that at all. It means you will not have the options that those who do ascend will have in the next round; you will not have the same level or scope of choices.

It is like you will be stuck in, say, grade school for your next series of lives. While all those who have dealt with their karmic agreements will graduate and move on to junior high, where they get to work with a much grander library, much finer teacher, much richer resources and much more interesting schoolmates.

Karma is so powerful – and disconcerting – because you do not know of it consciously; this is why there is such attention now to past-life regressions. You really do not have to do that, as fun as it is to see what other lives you played. In fact, you might very well become so enraptured over your old dramas that they will become the focus of your attention, and not what they represent.

The purpose is not the event, the purpose is to deal with the underlying issues.

Do not let yourself be so distracted in your journey of self. All you have to do is to look at your life here. You are creating events in your life now that mirror all those old dramas. Right now, you are being forced to deal with everything necessary to tell you what your issues – and obstacles – are in your path to mastery.

If you do this, you do not have to worry that at some point in time another karmic beast will jump up and bite you until you bleed.

Also, you do not have to obsessively study all the people in your life and ask yourself, 'Do I have a karmic tie with this one? What can my past lives tell me about that one? Will they be here to save me? Or damn me?'

Let us speak of this. There are many people in your lives at this time who were part of exchanges and events in earlier lives; or, they are part of your soul family and out of love they have agreed to come forth and share an event with you - to be a teacher and a student - in that which is termed a karmic tie. They might even be involved in the original relationship that stored this pocket of unresolved emotion on your body.

Understand you this, the nature of a karmic tie is nothing more nor less than an agreement between two people to facilitate the processing of this pocket of tar you have been carrying through unknown numbers of lives.

And, since a karmic tie is an agreement, also understand that all agreements can be changed at the will of the participants. You still are not a victim of any of this. Please remember that you are a face of God, and the nature of the universe is such that nothing can be done to any portion of the whole without its agreement

You entered your lives here with a structure of agreements that you chose, along with the agreements of others. You agreed to learn certain things; and the interplay between your soul and your personality – a creation of your soul – chooses how you learn those lessons.

Your soul negotiated with other souls to form a complex interweaving of agreements. These help create the classrooms that have enabled your soul, through the 'lens' of your personality and all of its particular – and peculiar – characteristics, to explore the issues it wanted to master and to learn the lessons it intended when it chose this life. This is extremely complicated...you might want to consider this a few moments before proceeding.

It is all of these agreements that form what you term karma. You need to know that you can change the agreements at any time, with certain conditions.

When the agreement is between two people, it is relatively simple to change. When it is between great numbers of people, it is far more difficult.

As we've said, there are physics to metaphysics, and it is complex to balance vast agreements – it is difficult to modify the inertia of mass social intention. They can be changed, but it takes a great deal of energy to do so. That energy can take the form of moderate events over time, or it may need to express itself in a massive event that triggers more immediate change – the kind of event that releases great amounts of energy in a very short time. Conflicts and events that capture the world's attention are examples of this; this includes wars and violent earth events and weather, among others.

Now, there have been rich prophecies throughout your history regarding this point in time. Prophecies that this planet would have many violent upheavals through shifts, rifts, cataclysms, all resulting in mass destruction.

At one time there were agreements in place for these. Some of these agreements have been changed, some have been withdrawn; those remaining can still be altered further or ended. And that fact is one of the greatest reasons why I am speaking to you. To help you understand that you are not victims, doomed to experience what has been foretold centuries earlier, without recourse, without options.

You simply need to know how to do this. All agreements can be changed; it is just that karmic agreements are more difficult to alter. For when you made these agreements you did so when you were fully present in your Godself; you were in your full power as creator. You said, 'I shall do all these things in my life and I shall bring you and you and you forth to help me in this and we shall do what we must; and we shall all work together to accomplish what we have agreed upon and we shall participate in these great events in order to accomplish our grand intentions and help the world understand certain truths.'

How can the you that is expressed by the personality you have chosen, a state of being that obviously is in much limitation, how can you change such powerful intentions set forth by your Godself?

You can when you create a clear connection with your soul.

How many of you have read that if you sit and concentrate and focus your mind on a goal, that if you put enough energy into visualizing a particular outcome that you can bend reality and create that goal? Many self-help books in your reality are based on this.

Fine, a child can concentrate all it wants, but it will not get to eat dinner consisting solely of chocolate ice cream. Only adults can create that. Do you understand what we are saying?

This is why such exercises do not work. Until you become your adult – fully connected with your Godself – no amount of kicking, screaming, bribing, or whining will get your unlimited self to do other than what it has chosen to do. You must understand that your soul is fully committed to creating events that continue to lead to the highest good of your being. And unlimited ice cream is probably not one of those.

The fundamental message in this is that you are the ones who are running your own lives...for your own highest good.

Life is not some nasty punchline imposed on you by some psychotic God that grades and judges you, who decides to play tricks and sets landmines in front of you. You have the power to change your lives because you are your own God, and nothing needs stand in your way.

All you need do, dear ones, is love yourselves as we do, and acknowledge the mastery within each of you and the God within each one of you.

You want to know how powerful you are? Look around your world. Look around your beautiful planet. Is she not grand. You created her, with your agreements, with your power, with your love...you created her.

You created all that is out there. You created the rocks, the wind, you created all of the beings that inhabit your lovely planet. You created everything and then you chose to live in it.

This is what life is all about. Living in it.

There are times when you bump up against your unlimited self and you engage in a will struggle, which you would typically feel in your throat - a cough, a constriction, a series of colds, and the like. When your personality starts resisting your soul, you begin creating an increasing series of situations designed to point out where you are out of alignment. You begin to see where you have chosen to play out your battles for growth and expansion.

You strengthen yourself with what you have chosen to overcome. If you were just the puppet of your soul, you would remain as children. Understand that your personality is a sovereign creation of your soul, to focus experience in order to explore certain aspects of reality.

You came here in your personality to experience those portions of the world that enable you to master the challenges you chose. This is why we are often silent, or mysterious at best, when your personality asks for answers, asks to be told of the future, and asks to be told what to do next. We cannot follow you around, commenting and directing every step, saying 'Walk here, step there, wear this, do that.' That would keep you as children.

You come to us and ask for advice and we must answer, 'What do you want to do? What do you think will be the consequences of that choice? What do you feel is for your highest good?'

It is in the finding out of who you are and what you want to do that you hone your skills, refine the connection to your sacred self, where you gain the power to create what you want.

As you step closer to harmony, you grow up. The child becomes the adult and steps into the full expression of your Godself. You find that part of yourself that you have forgotten about within you.

You can have chocolate ice cream any time you wish.

{ 12}

Knowing what to leave, knowing what to take

YOU ARE CREATORS, YOU ARE POWERFUL and you can do anything you wish. Hopefully, you are discovering that.

You have had glimpses of this so far, but it is time for you to stop playing around. It is time for you get on with all that you have agreed to do in this life.

Look at all you've done so far as your training for your great work.

Now you have to look back at all you've done in your lives and wonder if what you've done so far as been for your highest good or if it has been a vacation. Trust that it all has been for a purpose, but there are many paths to mastery. Some far more efficient than others.

Possibly you feel that you have to come to a point where you should cut yourselves off from all you have built in your old life. You look at the things you've done, the people you've known, the careers you've built and you wonder if it all was just prelude to a new and different future. Maybe you're in judgment of the inadequacies or ineptness of what you have known so far in your life and you feel you should let it all go in order to clear the decks and make ready for the 'new and improved' you.

What a sad waste that would be, to leave everything behind. This is not the case, you do not have to do this. If you believe you must, then you'll make yourself do this and there will be an enormous amount of discomfort in your future.

The purpose of your lives isn't simply to create and then destroy so you can make room to create again. It is to experience, to explore, to learn all that you possibly can in order to make yourselves ready for the next part of your lives.

Your life to this point has been to learn a diverse array of things - skills, beliefs, structures, desires, abilities, intentions – to build your expanded and enhanced hopes and dreams.

When you've finally achieved a state of competency in life, you might say, and you have created a clear and strong connection with your soul and you are ready to make your transition to the conscious road to mastery, you do not have to leave all your past behind. Take that which serves you into the next step in your evolution.

Why do you think you were brought to the point where you have spent so much of your energies doing all you've done. Regarding your work alone, think of all that you have learned and refined in order to achieve what you have in your working life. Just think of all you have gotten good at. Why should you throw all of that away?

It might be that you developed these skills in order to bring them into something else entirely...to help you manifest your grander dreams within a greater reality.

This is why you studied and you worked and you overcame endless frustrations. It is not so that you would feel an almost feverish relief at throwing it all away; it is to make you strong and accomplished within a particular group of knowledge and skills. And then to find a way to practice that which you so arduously learned and put it to use in a way that is more in keeping with the path of your soul.

Nothing is wasted in our reality, nothing ends or dies; it is simply transmuted into something better if that is your desire and if it facilitates your new path. Or, is it your intent to rather be stuck in one endless little loop. That is also within your power to create. You have already been stuck in some endless loops at some point in your life. This is all right, it taught you the meaning of waste and gave you the impetus to proceed more swiftly. How do you know what you can do well until you see what you have done so poorly.

What makes you venture into a new area where there is risk. Because you have finally gotten to the point where you are bored beyond existence – literally. So, you might choose another loop in order for you to find the impetus – because the alternative would be too stifling – to step off your cliff, to go into that which is dark, unknown, risky.

No one wants to go blindly where bullets might find them. Of course not. So you allow yourselves to get stuck; but even that is for the purpose of your higher path. Perhaps you wanted to immerse yourself in some experience, or decided to wait until something – or someone – else in your environment was ready for you. The point we are trying to make is that being stuck is not something to be in judgment about, it is something to accept as part of your path.

Would it not be easy if you, who created the structure of your lives, could go from point A to point B in a nice, neat, little dotted line in the shortest possible time. But how boring would that be. When you think of the weight of all the lives that you have created, if you journeyed the same straight line over and over and over again, what would be the point. How stifling.

Instead, you wanted to make it interesting; you wanted to take side trips and explore the byways of experience. Something caught your attention and you felt it would be fascinating to know more about that, so you bent your road a bit and took off for the hills. Or you met some intriguing people who seemed like they may have some insights and perspectives that could expand yours, so you joined them and helped them understand your unique point of view as well. All of this is your choice.

Do not be in judgment of anything you have done. Do not look back at any time of your life and feel you were lazy or inefficient or that you wasted time or lost progress, even if you went backwards for quite awhile. Each experience enriched you and added to the whole that is you. Do not beat yourself up for what you have done. You get so much pleasure out of beating your poor selves up…what is the point?

Every time you look in judgment on something that you have done, and think 'What a poor job, I wish I had done that better,' that means you are not fully considering that experience and learning all you can from it. You are not embracing it, you are not pulling it into your heart and accepting its essence and running it through your soul and expanding yourself from it.

When you think 'What an awful thing,' you are taking it, putting it outside of yourself, separating yourself from everything...anything...it could bring to you in knowledge and wisdom. You take your bricks, you get out your mortar; and with every row of the barricade you build, you say, 'How awful. How inept. How lame. How stupid.'

So you take that part of yourself that experienced that event and instead of learning from it, you judge it, you throw it away. And it is useless.

Because you have judged it inappropriate in your life, it may as well never have happened at all. What a waste of time and energy. For if you are indeed supposed learn something from that kind of experience, you will simply have to go through a similar one later.

Or, what if the experience was filled with great emotional pain, or rage, or fear. So, you start with the bricks, and then the iron bands to reinforce the bricks, and then the earth movers to bulldoze boulders in front of the wall – thinking that you will be safe from the pain or the anger of something you cannot understand, that you are afraid to assimilate into your being.

There is nothing you can put in front of those parts of yourself that you bricked up that will protect you from what waits behind the wall. For they are also you and, just like you, are infinitely powerful.

They will create an earthquake to move the boulders. They will rust the iron beams into nothingness, they will batter the brick into pieces, they will burn the house down to get through.

And you will not like that very much.

We suggest that you look back on all that you have lived - every experience, every relationship, every disappointment, every goal imagined and not met, every pain, every anger, every fear, every embarrassment. All those awful things you share with no one – those things you do not even write in your diary for fear someone might read it. Heaven forbid that you would be somehow diminished by revealing some part of yourself that everybody shares anyway.

Everything you have ever done and every part of yourself has been created ultimately for your highest purpose. You cannot put any of it behind you. You cannot put it away from you. You cannot separate it from you.

Those things you attempt to run from – all of those awful things – they will jump up and sink their fangs in your neck.

They will create patterns in front of you that you will not like.

They will mirror themselves in events, in relationships.

They will create voids in front of you in which there will be many people who would be more than happy to jump into that void and be your teacher – gleefully wielding the bat or slinging the rocks or mixing the tar. All to help you get it.

You would not like this, for some of the lessons could be quite painful. Whatever lesson you have attracted is not for the purpose of simply experiencing that event, it is for the purpose to get you to look at that which you have so arduously put behind all those barricades....so that you, in one sweep of your arm, can eliminate all the separation and pull it within you.

This is what a master does. You do not have to be the victim of your own inability to accept the world you have created.

Everything in your reality, you create. Why choose to be a victim of it. Every time you do not accept what you have created, every time you do not blend it within your being and take within it the mastery that you have searched for – that nugget within every event of knowledge that helps you grow – you are choosing to be a victim, you are denying the power of the lesson you created.

What do you think will happen when you turn away at the crucial moment in your lesson and do not look at the truth you chose to learn. You will create another, bigger, grander, harder lesson in front of you later.

Your unlimited self says, 'Get it?!' You answer, 'No, I can't, it's too hard, I can't.' So your higher self turns up the volume and says, 'All right, GET IT!!!???' And it gets louder and bigger and more fearsome in its size and strength.

How big does it need to be for you to get it? How massive does a lesson need to be for you to pay attention? Does it really need to become the equivalent of the Chrysler Building on your foot?

If your lessons get big enough...and if enough of you still do not choose to face your own truths, and you each put so much of yourselves behind those bars and barricades, and those personal demons all begin creating huge, vast lessons in order to finally get you to pay attention...then your blindness will work together as a community to create events that move the world.

So you manifest earthquakes. And you are surprised? You manifest great, torturous weather. And you are surprised?

You manifest armies that march into combat. And you are surprised and wonder how such things happened?

You even manifest great, crashing comets, worlds that collide...as you have in the past, right here in your own solar system.

If enough do not get it, imagine the awesome energies that you will create as a society, in order to make your world gets it.

That which you put behind bars will energize a reality that you will not like. You cannot blame us, you cannot blame God or fate or bad karma or luck. You cannot point to anyone outside yourselves. It is you doing this to you....by agreement.

You see, you cannot have a part of yourself that is separate from the rest of your being. You are each whole, infinite Gods. You will not allow yourself to say, 'This part of myself is far too uncomfortable to deal with. I'll put it out there where I do not have to deal with it and do not have to face the awful truths it tells me about myself. You be quiet, now.'

So you walk away and that unwanted, unrecognized, unrequited part of you grabs the flame thrower and it burns the door down. And it comes after you, except this time, it's grown teeth, because it's more determined than ever to get your attention. That is what happens.

You think you manage your lives by compartmentalizing all those pieces and parts of it, all those pieces and parts of your experience - your relationships, your work, your feelings, your dreams, your very thoughts, 'What an awful thought that is. I dare not think such a thing. I must be wicked indeed.'

So you put it away in a dark part of yourself, you are afraid that by recognizing it, you are encouraging it. That if you ignore it long enough, or cover it over with saccharin, pious thoughts you memorized from some dusty book, you will forget that it's there and be able to get on with your smooth, politically correct life. But there it remains, nevertheless, like the boogieman in the dark closet, sharpening its claws and waiting for the absolute perfect moment when it can leap out and create the most destruction in your life. It loves a good show...an important audience is its favorite condition.

It will not lie there like a sweet, docile, little puppy, waiting for you to pet it. For it is you and what would you do, if you were the part that was put in a dungeon and told to be a good little boy or girl? What would you do to get out? Maybe the better question is, what dreadful embarrassing destructive thing wouldn't you be willing to do to gain control and prevent ever being forced to hide, forgotten and damned in a hole much like hell?

You'd raise a war if necessary. A great war. A wonderful war. A creative, grand war. Because it would be fun, because that part is you, too – that nasty little thought that you are so ashamed of.

This is the purpose of all of your lives, to look at everything within you and your lives and accept it all. Take it in, embrace it, pull the darkness into the light, blend it all into one, glorious wholeness.

We started this discussion as though we were talking about a career shift; as though you had once learned business management, and then sometime in your life you thought, 'I do not wish to be a corporate flunky any longer, I wish to become a healer.' Well, maybe that ability to manage a business could be beneficial in your new path, too. Do not dismiss it and walk away from that expertise you so arduously learned.

But this is only a part of what we're talking about in your development and the evolution of your life.

Look at everything you have ever felt and thought. You had a thought or feeling that made you uncomfortable, so you put it away in judgment, 'I will not acknowledge such a thing, and I judge that part of me that thought such a thing to be an unhappy, angry, unworthy little child. I will not need such wretched little things in my new life. I wish to start over again, all new and shiny and pristine - without all of those awful things, those embarrassing, unworthy little things.'

You cannot do that, for they are each yourselves, and each part has their own flamethrower at the ready.

Bring all of them forward into your full awareness, not in judgment, but in acknowledgment. Look at them for all the insights they have to teach you about yourself. Look at them for clues about what you need to heal and what you need to mend in your heart and your history. Search them for the lessons they offer you, what they can bring into the new reality, the new future you are creating.

Most importantly, thank them. They were born for a reason. They are the children of your pain and your anger and your fear. And they came forth to help you face those painful, awful parts in your being and your life and to dissolve the toxins and the venom and to embrace them fully into the light of your soul.

After that, the rest will be easy.

Look at all the skills you have learned. If you do not like where you have applied them, then apply them somewhere else.

Look at the emotional tools you evolved. It you do not like how you applied them in your relationships, then apply them differently, or forgive yourself and absolve them. Do not shut them away.

Look at your pictures, your expectations of yourself. You have way too many. The desire to strive for that which is better is admirable; to think you are inept where you are, or incompetent if you do not reach your expectations is not. Judgments improve nothing, excuse nothing. You think you need to judge yourself because you feel everyone else does...and you are busy judging them because you think they are in judgment of you.

If someone is indeed judging you, why should you buy into their need to do so. You think you will preempt their judgment by jumping ahead of them and judging yourself more than even they did?

You grew up in a maze of judgments created by your parents not simply to shape your development, but to control you. And after you grew up you had absorbed so much of their judgment that you in effect carry your parents within you at all times. You have breathed them and their thought-forms in. It is time to let them go and find your own view of self.

You are not lazy, you are not stupid, you are not unethical, you do not have bad taste, you do not have bad friends, you do not have dumb thoughts. You are not the gawky teenager who reveled in a room heaped with old clothes. You are not the little kid who embarrassed him or herself on the playground, or the last child picked during team-up.

You grew through all of that and found your strengths and exercised your prerogatives and tried and tested and failed and retried and accomplished and changed and grew. And lived. Your life. Your life. You found a path that brought you here, now, holding this book, searching for a reality beyond the existence you have known, a reality that would lead to mastery, to remembering the Godself within.

How can you judge yourself in the face of all that you've known and tried? Why should you, what purpose does it serve?

Every time you judge yourself, you're putting a part of yourself behind the wall where it will contort out of grief and anger at being so judged and dismissed. It will find a way to get out and burn your house down.

Trust me, I am not one of those old men in golden robes sitting in front of a great carved dais, who rails against you and says you are weak, you are lacking, you were born in sin and live in inadequacy and die in shame.

I tell you you are wondrous, you are light, you are God.

You cannot accept this because you are afraid to accept it. You are afraid to say, 'I am a wonderful being, I am God. And I created this great world and I love myself because of it.' Because you are afraid of sounding foolish and vain and arrogant.

That is none of those things. Foolish is saying, 'I don't know if I could possibly love myself, I'm such an idiot.' Vain is, 'Of all that's beautiful, I am the most beautiful and the most special.' Arrogant is, 'All of this exists to serve me, for I am not simply one of the Gods, I am the center, and God knows, the world exists to make me happy.'

You are not guilty of any of these, except maybe the first...at times. Look around in pride at your lives, look around at all you've done, look at the hardships you have chosen. Look at these, embrace these, love all of them and thank them.

Look at all the things you have judged stupid that you have done, 'Wasn't it wondrous I had the courage to do all that I've done in my life. Hasn't it all been extraordinary. I love myself because of this and I love myself for being a part of this great reality and this great world. I look at every person in front of me and I see their God that reflects me within them. I look at them in joy, and I enjoy them.'

That is how you find joy. You might even say this out loud to yourself in a mirror. If rituals and affirmations help you uncover your creative abilities, this one is a powerful one.

Acknowledge everything you are, acknowledge everything you have done. Be not in judgment, be not in torment, do not think you are lacking. You are what you are, you did what you needed to do to become that which you are. Choose to accept that. It is as simple as that.

Some part of you is likely sitting here wondering, 'Why am I here? What is my life's purpose? Why did I choose this? Where am I supposed to go? What am I supposed to do? How can I be of service?'

You look at your lives and you try to find out what you are supposed to be here for, and you are perplexed. 'I know I chose something better than this. Can this be all? This doesn't feel right, this doesn't make me joyful. Why am I here?'

And sometimes your lives give you pain, sometimes you experience things that are discomforting. You have parts that feel terrible. It is like the joke in your reality when you go to a doctor, 'Doctor, it hurts when I do this.' 'Then don't do this,' the doctor replies.

So we tell you, if your life hurts, don't do it. If it feels right, do more of it. The challenge is to make sure you can tell the difference between your soul and your child who is doing the feeling. It is the path to mastery we've talked about that prepares you for that ultimate discernment.

Look at your lives. What gives you joy? In that you will find your purpose, or at least a gem, a grain, a microbe of your purpose.

Where does the heart lead you, what makes your heart happy? Where are your passions, what do your feelings tell you? What have you done, that when you have done it, you lost all sense of time passing?

Look back at every job you ever had; you worked there by your agreement to learn something, to experience something. A skill? Knowledge? An understanding of the dynamic of the exchange of energy in your commerce. What did you like most about that job, what did you like least. What made you feel productive. What didn't work. What sticks with you. What did you hate. Think about all of these things and ask yourself why.

Take what you discover from all this and learn from it. Don't file it under old history and forget about it, don't waste all the time and energy you put into it.

Do this with all the experiences in your life. There will be a thread - those things sharing some property, some character that attracted your fancy. Or it will be a little building block with an edge that fits just so, and another building block, and another. You start putting these all together and your path will begin to be evident.

You will begin to understand something of the overarching intention of your life. You will begin to see the reason why you chose to be here.

You will see what stirs your passion. And once you know what is in your heart, and you become integrated, whole, then you will become closer, more connected to your soul within you, the sacred Godself who will access the energies to bring to you those opportunities enabling you to use all those things you have learned.

Once you have done this, you do not have to sit and wonder what you need to do next. Your job is to fully understand yourself. We will bring you the opportunities to express that which is you wonderfully well.

Your job is not to look through the yellow pages to find out what should you do next with your life. Your job is to open up your heart and look at your lives, look at every part of your lives with a magnifying glass.

If you come across a door, open it. If you come across a wall, knock it down. Do whatever it takes to open all the dark, closed parts of your being. Stand with courage and conviction and face whatever comes forth in this internal journey of discovery. Do not be afraid of anything you find. If you do not approach those unwanted and discarded portions of yourself and of your history, they will approach you, and you won't like that nearly as much. The difficult will become overwhelming. The unpleasant, torturous. The unsettling, fearsome indeed.

But if you explore and embrace your entire being, you will begin to see immediate changes in your life. You will begin to see your life's purpose and you will begin to attract events and opportunities in your life that will facilitate that purpose.

So after all this difficult self-examination, finally, you get to this point in your life where you are ready to make that great step and leap into your new and improved future...you draw this line and you say, 'All right, I'm ready. So I will let go of all of the old, unserving me and step over.'

Now what? There's all that you left behind that could be of service in your new life, talents and knowledge and insights and expertise that, if applied in slightly different ways within different contexts, would enable you to achieve your passions and manifest your purpose.

The quandary is to know what to take with you, and what to leave behind. You ask how will you know which is which. Well, how do you think you know such things? You are the masters, learn your mastery.

You know by asking yourself, by looking inside yourself. You ask your heart, you look at your life. You have made many choices based on what you felt was correct. Look at those choices and the consequences of those choices. Evaluate which choices created positive results, and which led to negative outcomes. Such a process will tell you much about what works for you, and will help you determine your next, most appropriate choices.

Does that seem like an enormous amount of work? So instead you buy endless self-help books and pour over them for clues. You ask your psychiatrists for assessment. You look for spiritual gurus to give you instant insight and direction. You come to us and ask our advice, 'What should I do now? Where should I go? What's going to happen next? Which option should I choose?'

Why blindly offer up your sovereignty to someone else so easily. Do you really want us to run your lives? If you did - if we did - you would be trading mastery for comfort, you would be remaining as a child and acting as a puppet.

You like to complain. If we don't give you enough advice, you demand why are we here. If we give you advice you don't like, you accuse us of telling you what to do.

The human condition is that you like to complain. If you can complain, you can make it someone else's fault.

But this is your life...you are living the results of your choices. But you think that if you complain about something, you can blame someone, make them responsible for what happened. 'It's not me, it's not my fault. They did it!'

Well, you did, too. It was you. You did all of it.

You constructed your life and all that has been in it to teach yourself many things and give you many skills, so that when you move into your new future, you can step confidently, knowing what you are to carry and what you are to let go of.

When a child doesn't know what to do, a child wants to be given all the easy answers, wants to have everything without having to prioritize anything. It wants to carry everything and then it asks for help carrying it all. And, oh by the way, where did you put my blue blanket?

There's a lot more to life than that. You are here to become masters. You are not here to become stuck behind those little walls that will keep you forever children – whining, complaining, unable to access the energies of the universe to accomplish all that you desire, unable to find the passion and the mastery that will create your joy.

You are grand beings. You are learning how to work with the light and you are beginning to suspect that you have a far greater purpose in your reality than you ever imagined.

But there's a part of yourself that breathed in all those judgments around you and said, 'It cannot be. I am not worthy. It is far too silly an idea to think that I, who could not even keep my room picked up, am supposed to be one of those to save the planet.'

Well, if you don't even try, what about those who cannot keep their rooms picked up still? If you do not know how to become the teachers, how do you expect them to learn? You are the advanced guard.

Now there are many who are far more advanced than you, and beyond them, and beyond them. And then behind you, there are infinite armies of those desperately looking for help.

This is your time. Why do you think that you chose to be incarnate in this place, at this time? This is the time that you've all chosen to live when and where all the rules are changing. It is very hard, harder than it has ever been, but somebody has to do it, and this is what all of your lives have been in preparation for.

This is why you are each and all creating such great events surrounding you.

Deal with them now. Let the walls come crashing down. Blend all of this within you, embrace all that you've created in this life to mirror all those parts of yourself that you have shut away out of pain and fear and judgment. And once you do that, you will be great luminous beings.

This does not mean this process is pleasant. In fact we know how awful it is, how much it hurts, how frustrating. You wonder if there is an end to all of this, if you will ever finally reach a state where you can stop with the processing already and get on with the better, grander more satisfying portion of your life. Yes.

Now the question we ask you is what do you want that portion to be?

What kind of life do you want? Do you want the happy ending? So be it. Do you want catastrophe? So be it. It is in your province. Your choice.

The rest of your life will be determined by how well you do all of it up to the point where you make a conscious choice to begin your new future, where you choose what to bring with you, what to leave behind. Knowing that when you step over, you have prepared yourself well.

{ 13}

Relationships, that perfect reflection of you

THIS IS THE TIME WE HAVE SAID you are being asked to deal with those parts that you were very good at hiding from.

If you are too encumbered with this burden of dark, unhappy little demons within you, if you are too laden down with the armor of fear and anger, with the need to separate yourself from those parts you cannot face, how do you expect to 'graduate' from this third-dimensional reality? How do you expect to move up with your great planet during what is by some called the ascension?

Let us talk about this...'moving on up,' so to speak. There is judgment in that. In truth, it is not ascension, it is simply a transition to a 'faster' expression of the energetics of the infinite light.

All reality, as we have explained, consists of energy in a state of vibration - tiny little particles of light whirling around other tiny little particles of light at a certain frequency of vibration. There are twelve 'levels' – or states – of vibration, each level supporting and enhancing the next level. The twelfth level is the composite of the first eleven levels; it is this vibration that encompasses all beingness, and has been described as the universal 'Ommm' of unconditional love – all thought, all awareness, all experience, full acceptance without condition or qualification, total allowing of beingness. The perfection and totality of All That Is.

Now, as the result of this transition, your planet will assume a faster state of vibration, as will all of you who accompany her. When you become a faster expression of energy, you access greater amounts and frequencies of the universal Ommm, the spaces in your cells expand and you enjoy some specific enhancements in the potential of how you manifest your intentions as a being.

You will not be limited by third-dimensional reality, third-dimensional rules. You can then move along any lines of light you will have learned to access and project.

Time will not limit you. Know you what time is? It is an artificial construct, a function of certain dimensional levels, to organize your experience.

You are not bound by this if you reach beyond the limited mind to the unlimited self. Nor will you be bound by space. That is also a means of organizing experience.

Time allows the choices you make to move through space, enabling you to see the consequences of those choices, and thus experience the manifest act of a creator.

Outside of the 'lower' dimensions (no judgment there, truly, merely a description of level of vibration, and therefore, potential), we are not bound by such things as time and space. What need us to organize our intentions in so linear a manner, when we can bend time and fold experience back on itself and make the potential expression of cause and effect a bit more intriguing. You are learning how to do this, to speed and slow time, to alter the inertia of third-dimensional reality with the strength of your will, a function of your divine intentions.

To do this, to achieve this advanced state of expression, you have to refine your expression of self in the third dimension and clear yourself of all the 'heavier' thoughtforms that will hold you back. You have to let go of those old pictures and the old pockets of beliefs and pain, the old stifling structures, the anger and pain and fear that no longer serve you. This is the time to face yourself. When you feel raw and in sorrow and in fear, you put yourselves in judgment, 'What have I done wrong, what am I doing wrong to feel this?'

What you are learning to do is to face with strength and courage and clarity the causes and effects of your lives. As you do that, you allow the wisdom of what you have collected with all your efforts to be enfolded within you.

Everyone who has gone through great sorrow – the sorrow so deep in your spirit, the dark night of your soul – knows that it takes your control away. That is not such a bad thing. In fact it is very helpful in your evolution.

What is control? The walls and barriers, and the armor and the bricks and the boulders that you put out to protect yourself. It is the vain attempt to protect yourself from risk, from failure. Anyone who is so averse to failure will never put themselves in a position to learn very much. Those of you who ski know that if you do not fall down occasionally, you are not trying very hard. So it is with life.

If you put so much of your energy into controlling your environment, controlling any possible outcomes in order to protect yourself from harm or embarrassment, you will never explore much that is new. You cannot control the unknown.

But perhaps the real thing you are trying to control is yourself. And is that not a foolish vanity as well? You cannot protect yourself from yourself. You always know exactly what it takes to get to you.

So you learn to face all that, to find ways to let go of the need to control all in your lives. You learn to face those parts of yourself that were in so much fear, that required so much control, and you love them into wholeness. That is what we are here to help you do. This is why you are here and this is why we have come, to look at the wonder of you, and acknowledge what you have done here surrounded by all this limitation – all that you have chosen in your lives, all that you have committed to, all you have experienced.

We are here to tell you that you did it out of love, not out of punishment, not out of fear. You did it out of love – love for the essence of you that is a face of God, love of that part of yourself that you see in everyone. We are here to help you activate that part so that you can then feel the love within yourself for yourself...for all of yourself.

You will see the God that is within each one of you, the Godself that is the essence of your soul, that you share with everyone on this planet, with everyone who has ever been, is, shall be...anywhere, anywhen.

You can learn at look at another person and say, 'I see that sacred essence of God in you, I see that part that we share in you, I see a portion of me behind your eyes. We are not separate, we are simply different faces of the One.' And when you know that, when you feel that, all that you know and feel becomes a source of joy.

We have talked about how you clear yourself, how you find your heart, how you feel what you feel with courage. We have talked about karma, which is nothing more than those pockets of things you had not mastered that you carried forward with you into this life from others.

Now, we will talk about relationships.

You know, relationships...the solution you think will make you happy if you just find the right one.

Not so.

A relationship will simply magnify within you all that you have not done. So, why have any relationships at all? Why not live your life as the strong, silent type, why not live in isolation, on a mountaintop, contemplating one's navel.

Of all the rich experiences that are available in this life, why would one choose such sterile limitation. It is an unhealthy, unserving and un-holy idea.

We have explained how you reach where you want to go in this reality – by living your lives, by living every step of every day. You chose your flesh, love it, enjoy it. You chose your lives, live them. You chose this planet, walk upon it, love it.

And you chose to live within a society filled with diverse individuals, each with a unique point of view, each with a particular – and at times peculiar – way of expressing their soul. Is that not wonderful? What better way to learn how to practice the highest state of God by learning to accept all of the rich – and at times irritating – diversity around you.

And...most importantly...what better way to learn about yourself than by experiencing your differing responses to all the different individuals that surround you every day of your life.

Relationships tell you more about yourself than sitting in a dark room contemplating colors in order to tune your chakras ever will. For you see magnified in the person staring back at you, all of your faults and all of your gifts.

The quality of your relationships is entirely dependent upon the quality of your own spiritual growth.

For you are the creators and everything outside of yourself reflects that which is within yourself. There is nothing outside of you, including all of your relationships.

Understand that the purpose of relationships is to enhance your experience on this reality. If relationships were not critical in exploring the infinite potential of beingness, God would never have become other than the One.

You all need each other. This is why you are here. If you did not need any other being, you would not have chosen to be in this great world and would have chosen another type of existence in another type of reality, for that is your prerogative.

That is the purpose of being here, to explore who and what you are in community with others, to explore that fine line between your own wishes and sovereignty, and the wishes and sovereignty of others. You can't truly know what is appropriate for you without testing what is inappropriate. You can't know how you are doing in your spiritual evolution without seeing the consequences of your choices; and an excellent way to see that is by how they affect others.

So, in order to work out your own issues, you attract others into your environment. The interaction of your face with their face, and your issues with their issues, accommodating, melding, opening your heart to feel another, to transcend the illusion of separation on this plane...this is why you chose to be here and you cannot do it sitting in a room concentrating on colors, listening to pretty music, reading your clever books.

You chose to be here to be in a community, to relate one to another to another; so that in another's eyes, you can see a reflection of yourself, and see better who you are.

If someone angers you, they are not forcing you to feel anger. They are holding up a mirror of that part of yourself you do not like very much, that part of yourself you want to put back behind your dungeon door. A great service, that.

When you look into another's eyes and you see the regard they have for you, you see acceptance for all you are and are not – unconditional love – you are looking at that part of yourself which is capable of feeling this.

Know the story of creation? It is a simple one. God was One, and that One was All. But how boring that was. Even God cannot experience much if being One is all there is.

So, God contemplated itself and then became 'more.' After all, when there are more beings, there are more options, aren't there? But the essential nature of divine intention is to explore and experience all that possibly can be. So 'more' became too limiting. God therefore became 'many.'

The angelic plane was born. And 'dark' was born – not as a punishment for those that did not do well, but to enhance the experience of All. Dark is not evil – that is a judgment you have projected onto it. Dark is simply definition, it allows light to define its existence. Dark is challenge. When you have to play against the dark, you learn a lot more about the capabilities of the light.

Male and female were born, and that made it very interesting indeed. Again, the purpose...not to separate or create a greater or lesser expression of God, but to expand experience, to explore different aspects of experience.

And that certainly is the purpose of relationships – to expand experience, to enlarge awareness. Not to use as a drug, not to fill your time and distract you from self, not to hide from who you are, naked in that empty room, certainly not to use as you use your televisions shows – to mindlessly entertain and lose your sense of self. Not to use as something that will deaden the pain or the sorrow or the anguish or the loneliness you feel.

That is not the purpose of relationships.

If you treat your relationships that way, you are looking at this other person and telling them, 'It is your job to make me happy. And if you do not, I will hate you and punish you.'

What a wretched thing to do to yourself and to another. That's not a relationship, that's a punishment.

You cannot look at a relationship as something that will fix all of the holes your parents left in you, that other lovers left in you, that life left in you.

You cannot use your relationships to make you feel clever, when you in fact feel stupid.

You cannot use a relationship to make you feel warm, when you are chilled by an inability to open your heart to the warmth of another.

You cannot use your relationships like a tropical resort. 'I will visit them when I need to feel good and then, when it is too much responsibility or bother, I will leave and come back later, when the coast is clear.'

A relationship is the ability to face someone and say, 'It is good to meet you, it is good to meet that part in you that is also in me. Thank you for bringing me that lovely and loving view.' And then it is stepping back with a warm smile and waiting to see what happens.

It is not dumping all of your overwhelming boxes and burdens of expectations at the other's feet and saying, 'Ok, now what are you going to do for me? How are you going to fix me? What will you do to make me happy?'

You cannot bribe another person to make you feel whole. You cannot tell them, 'If you do this for me, then I will do that for you.'

That's not a relationship. That's a barter. You cannot bargain for love.

Where is the relationship in that? That is an 'expecting'-ship. There is no giving, there is no sharing, no revelation or expansion, no communion. You use your relationships at times like bandages.

Relationships expand the universe for you. If you cannot look at another person and see in that one the sacred Godself, and love it and accept it, how can you expect to look within yourself and love yourself for all you are and, more importantly, for all you are not.

Relationships are not something to be used as a test. 'How lovable am I? What will you do to show me how lovable I am?'

Relationships are not expectations or questions. Relationships are acceptances.

It is looking at another and saying, 'Thank you. Thank you for helping me be a better me, for helping me see I am – like you – a sacred face of God.'

Relationships are also not searching the world high and low, looking for what you like to call your 'twin flame' or your 'soulmate,' or any other part that you believe will make you whole. 'I am incomplete without that one, magical person who will come in and fill all my holes up and make me happy.'

What an awful burden that is on anyone.

Yes, there are twin flames, but they are not your idealized romantic partner for all time, through all time.

They are the other polarity of energy of your being – that other one who was formed when you split into the duality of male and female in order to be incarnate here, back when time was much, much younger. But then understand that each of you continued to split into more beings to create more options of experience. So your twin flame might now be the equivalent of a small army – in both genders – and each one of you has experienced many many existences that will have effected the nature of who you are. The 'fit' will no longer be two halves of a whole. It will be far more interesting.

You were not formed to be the one, true romantic mate of each other. Twin flames were created as part of your desire to experience All That Is. What one experiences, the others also understand – though not necessarily on a conscious level.

Also know that you are not brought together lightly. When you are, it is to be the teacher of a lesson that you will simply not accept in any other way, from any other teacher.

Do not spend your lives searching high and low for a twin flame. Know that if your other is truly in this life, and you have agreed to come together for whatever purpose, there is nothing that can keep you apart. Though in truth, you might not find the experience of coming together the perfect union you fantasize.

It is far more likely to be the greatest challenge of your life. For the other one has come to ensure – by any means necessary – that you will get a critical lesson in your evolution.

Now, soulmates are those who are from your soul family – the large group of entities formed by the splitting and splitting and splitting again and again of a particular component of awareness within the evolution from God the One into God the Many. They contain a diverse range of harmonics in affinity, much broader than those expressed in the evolution of the twin flames.

Soulmates are those who have come forth within this life – by mutual agreement – to be here when you need support, at an agreed-upon time, for an agreed-upon experience. Soulmates come and go during your lives, and there are many who are here for you, and for many different purposes...not simply as romantic playmates to push back the loneliness.

The idea that there is but one, single person on the planet who is designed to be your mate, with whom you can share a life and create an ecstasy of joy and belonging is cruel. Do you think that the universe would be so heartless as to put on this great planet only one capable of sharing happiness with you. And that your whole life must be as a detective to find that one. Would it not be awful if one was four and the other was eighty. It does not work that way.

There are many who are here from your soul family to be of service. This is all by agreement. You come together at times in your lives when you think, 'Wouldn't this be lovely? I come forth to you at a time when you need to learn something, and I need to learn something from you. So this is our agreement and we come together and we live the agreement and then it is free will. Now, what do we wish to do? Do we wish to commit? Do we wish to try something else, someone else?'

There is no judgment in this. Only experience.

There are many who are here with whom you can share a rich and satisfying partnership on every possible level. There are those with whom you can explore dizzying heights of love and ecstasy, and is that not wondrous.

But it is not the cosmic jigsaw puzzle in which there is only one.

Please hear this fully and carefully: Your ability to find this incredible happiness and joy with another person is not because you have found the right needle in the infinite hay stack.

It is because you have found that ability within yourself.

When you find within you the ability to express joy and to love yourself, you will then attract to you like a great cosmic magnet, someone whose time it is to be activated in your life in order to share the joy, each with the other.

Think about this. Absorb this. Immerse yourselves in this truth, for once you are fully one with it, you will be able to create it.

If you think that you go through your lives searching for the one person, 'Will you be the one who will help me find joy?' you bring enormous expectations of their behavior, you come equipped with all sorts of baggage that you expect them to carry for you.

Instead, they will learn to hate you, because they will most certainly feel it is not a love without condition. It is very conditional; you will not love them unless they are nice to you all the time, unless they salve your wounds and boost your flagging spirits. It has become a negotiation. It is a business agreement. It is not a relationship of the heart.

Instead, if you learn to love yourself and see within you the God in each of you, and you see the glory, the infinity of love that you have forgotten and covered over in all of your lives – the things you have not been able to process yet – once you uncover that, you will then activate the one who will come forth into your life and say, 'I know you. You are wonderful. Thank you.'

Because this partnership will then not be an addiction. It will not be a crutch, nor a bandage, nor a wheelchair. It will be a meeting of giants, a union of Gods. And in this union of Gods, anything is possible.

So the task is not to go out there and search the world over with a flashlight and binoculars.

The task is to be who you are, to have a clear connection between your personality and your soul, to be fully in your Godself. And then to trust that when you are so integrated, the most amazing series of events will begin to happen. Such incredible coincidences will astound you that will bring this perfect, magical person in front of your face, and into your life.

And you will know love. Deep, joy-filled, unconditional love.

You will finally know what we feel for you. We tell you the universe is not random, nor cold, nor cruel. It is designed to help you master cause and effect, learning how to make the kind of choices in your life that help you to understand, and then to live in the state of unconditional love.

We so love you. If we did not, and if this life were simply a punishment, why ever would those of us who learned to fly from jumping off our own cliffs, why should we ever come back here to help you.

If you were the awful, puny people that so many have told you that you are, we would flee like those birds in your sky, as far away from here as is possible. If you finally managed to escape the penitentiary, would you ever come back to visit and hold the hands of those who remain?

This is a fascinating place and you are amazing beings, and we come here for we want to expand your joy. For as your joy is expanded, so is the joy of everyone in the universe. We feel it and are ennobled by you, we are blessed by you.

This is what living fully in the infinite light of the universe does for you. Do you find yourself wondering where we live?

What it looks like? Are there great pillars and posts, marble columns, harp music and beautiful confections?

We exist within the living light – that infinite glow of the love, the universal Ommm that is shared by all beings. That is where our home is. And, as I've said, we do not know time as you do. We simply are, and we manifest that beingness wherever we wish to be….anytime, anyplace, instantly. We can be everywhere and we can be nowhere – as you would imagine 'where' and 'when' are.

It is not possible to explain to a mind bound at this time in limited third-dimensional reality that which is unlimited and exists in much higher dimensional state of being. Just know that we evolve as you do; there are some correlations. When you ascend and you quicken, you are simply given more choices.

You do not need to come back here to learn; you can if you wish, that is your choice. You can come back incarnate, fully realized, which is how I lived many of my lives here, as teachers planting those little seeds of awareness.

You can come back as what you call an ascended master – in energy only – and do your work as a teacher and guide. You can choose the kind of work you wish to do, based on what you enjoy and on the capabilities you have created with the body of your experience. You can speak to others as I do.

You can simply add to the healing frequencies of the universe; or help manifest the events called forth through agreement, if you are intrigued by the physical workings of reality and you want to be a technician. There are vast computers – a metaphor of course – that run our universe, and you can work with them to facilitate the structure of reality. There are many levels of experience and manifestation of your divine intentions to express your Godself.

Just know that beyond the levels of this life, your choices are simply grander, more infinite.

You can do anything, anywhere, anywhen you wish. If you like the trappings of a certain life, you can manifest it. You can go back and visit that time, you can carry aspects of that with you so that others can respond to it, an effective way to engage the personalities of those you come to help.

Why do you think those aspects of God who come back as guides, ascended masters, appear to be male or female? Understand that when you get beyond a certain level of reality, you are a fully integrated expression of your potential within God. You are not a male or a female any more. You simply are.

An interesting concept to you, we imagine.

At that level, we are no longer an age, yet why does a guide appear as an old man, or woman, or child. Why do they carry the name of only one of their incarnations. Why do some let go of their earthly experiences and step back to an earlier existence and take a star name, as I have. It is because there is pleasure in being. It doesn't matter who you are or what you've been, it only matters what serves your intention at that moment in your existence.

You have choices…is not that exciting? Do you now feel less bound by those sorrows that surrounded your heart and made you feel there was nothing more that was better? Do you now feel some part of the excitement of the infinite? Are you not in some way stirred by the idea that anything is possible, that you can accomplish universes?

This realization will help awaken more of you. You have found this book because you have asked for an acceleration.

You will have more and more of your random DNA reconnected, and the more that takes place, the smarter you will become, the more you will access those parts of your mind that are outside of your limited experience, and you will begin to embrace much higher frequencies of energy and manifest much greater realities.

You will experience such grand creative leaps. Your minds will be so expanded with the ability to go beyond your linear microsteps of limited experience.

Is this not a joyful message? Does this make your heart happier, fuller.

You can become that which will attract to you that magical being who will recognize the sacred Godself within, who will see the impossible journey you have taken in your life to reach that state of connection, who will applaud every step and love you for all that you are and all that you have done.

And you will be that magical being who will do the same for your mate.

You will also attract to you the work that will make your heart happy, that allows a more comprehensive expression of the stronger, more integrated wholeness you have achieved, that will attract to you whatever material manifestations in your life you wish.

And that's what all of this work will bring to you. It will bring your mastery.

It will bring you to a life filled with love.

{ 14 }

What next?

AFTER ALL OF THIS, do you understand who you are and why you are here?

Have you found your answers to your hardest questions:

How to find joy. How to heal your wounded selves. How to open your compassionate hearts. How to find your highest expression of self.

How to heal those parts of yourself that you have carried with you through so many lives, to help you release karmic agreements as easily and painlessly as possible.

To understand all of the work, all of the awareness, all of the exploration of your world. To understand why you are here.

All this is simple...

So that you will achieve your mastery of self and go out and spread your loving energy through your loving hearts and help others achieve the same transcendent state. So that you will save your world.

This is your gift, and this is why you are here.

Finally, we have to say to you, 'What next?'

When you finish these pages, put the book down and go forward from here in your lives, you will take that which is the essential part of yourself, which has been tuned, which has been strengthened and opened fully, so that you can then do all you can to reach your mastery and help others.

This does not mean you have to stand in front of groups lecturing, trying to push people into a greater understanding of themselves and reality. It means that you can now proceed on your path with your heart wide open, projecting great, healing quantities of unconditional love through your expanded, expansive hearts to the world.

When you do this, you can do anything.

Once you know how to open your heart to the energy of All, you become a conduit of the energies of healing, of empowerment, of infinite knowledge to everyone in your planet.

You do not have to study this, your lives are your classroom. Your experience is your dissertation. All of your lives brought you to this point in your evolution.

And, dear ones, you have done it, you've graduated. You've achieved a state of awareness that in effect places you on the edge of a great cliff. Below you are incredible experiences just waiting for your arrival.

From this moment on, your lives will change. All you need do is make the leap and use your new wings.

You will be dazzled by the beauty of the landscapes that stretch in front of you. You will be intoxicated by the feeling of power and mastery as you soar on the winds of energy, moving where you will.

This does not mean you can move into fantasyland, and manifest nothing but chocolate ice cream. That tropical resort is a fine place to go for a weekend; after a lifetime it gets boring, and you get stupid and you get lazy. It is not a master's choice.

What does it mean to go forward from here? It means to live your lives to the fullest. Open your hearts to more energy, to more beingness, to more awareness, more experience, to fullness.

Think what makes a full life.

Not a little playground. It takes great mountains and deserts and oceans and rivers and sun and rain and rainbows. It is being where you are and loving it. It is knowing your place in the universe and glorying in the possibilities.

Once you know who you are, there is nothing you cannot do. There's nothing you cannot go out and accomplish. And once you understand the gift of all the laughter, and the love, and the sorrow, and the anger, you understand the richness of all of this, and what they all bring you. For this is why you are here. To feel all of it.

What great messengers your emotions are, telling you everything you need to know of your reality.

So you take all of this, you go forth, and you become grander still. Turning the volume up means you become a greater beacon – burning brighter, hotter, casting more light to all around you.

You reach out, you can touch all. Light knows no boundaries. It knows no separation. Nothing stands in front of light, nothing. Certainly not the darkness.

All of the darkness you fear, all of the darkness that makes you tremble, nothing stands in front of the light. All is healed. All is empowered. All is brought to an understanding of who and what it is. The light can move anything, accomplish anything. It creates rainbows.

When you take the fullness of light, think of all you can do with it. Every vibration of every form of consciousness is made of light. When it becomes a rainbow, it refracts itself into a dazzling array of vibrations - the color spectrum you see, and vast ones that are invisible to your human eyes. They are all there. Every one is different.

It is this amazing array that makes your planet remarkable. A fantastic collection of unique expressions of the infinite light.

You are each one of you different, unique, special, blessed. Each one of you is a different face of the light, a crucial aspect of the light. If we could combine every one of you in the universe, we would recreate the One, the singular, perfect light of the original God, the ultimate expression of unconditional love.

Without any one of you, it would not be complete. You are each essential to All That Is. Without you, there would be a hole, an incompleteness. Nothing else could fill it.

This is who you are, this is what you are. Light, love made manifest.

Once you understand this, once you feel this within your heart, you can access this unlimited light, the energy, the building block of all reality, take it out and do with it what you will. Exactly what you will.

Once you become aware, once you wake up your grander Godself within, there is nothing you cannot do.

You have come here to these lives to create experiences, to bring you back to the awareness, to enjoy the ecstatic moment when you remember the infinite joy of your Godself. And in all of these tasks, and all of the places you have gone throughout all of your lives, think of all that you have learned, and brought to the One. Think of how much your efforts have added to the grander understanding of All.

You ask, if you are unlimited God, why did you choose to do this to yourselves, to come here and experience all of this in limitation – the frustrations, the difficulties, the pain, the awful lives. Because you wanted to experience more. You wanted to experience being a creator by creating your own lives.

The compelling nature of life is to expand life. To grow. To experience more. To create.

Nothing is static. Nothing remains the same. Nothing dies.

You came down upon that which you created, this planet you created, the bodies you created, and then you chose to inhabit them, because it looked so joy-filled an experience.

But in these lives you created so well, you became like actors who were lost in your roles. You forgot that there is more.

So you've lived all of these lives to bring you back to the full awareness that there is more.

And here you are, paying attention, for that is why you found this book. You are all grander, greater, richer, vaster. You are all coming into your unlimited selves.

What you have asked for, you will begin to manifest. Do not doubt that.

Just know it may not manifest itself according to your limited pictures, from your limited minds. Be open to experiences, possibilities that are grander than you can imagine at this time. Do not limit your transformation by saying it must proceed in a certain way. Be open to all possibilities.

The amount of the light that can come through you will be as infinite as your open mind and your open heart. Do not let it be bound by small expectations.

Anything is possible, anything. And once you believe that anything is possible, then you are freeing that creative part in yourself to make it so.

All the rules are off. What you believe, you manifest. What you feel, your heart will access. The more you allow yourself to feel, the more you will be able to access that energy that you can use to create all of your beliefs.

So, make your beliefs grand ones.

We will give you everything you need if you believe in yourself. Jump off your cliff, be not afraid of that. We will not let you fall. Spirit loves courage. When you have a brave heart, it is because you are fully in trust.

To be in trust means you are fully integrated with your Godself.

Do not go around with little safety nets. If you put all of your energy into creating safety nets, what are you telling the universe – that you need to be protected, like a child needs safety wheels? You are saying that you do not trust that you will learn how to fly, you do not trust us not to let you fall.

Throw your safety nets away. Be not afraid. Be in trust, be in love, love yourselves, and there is nothing you cannot do.

The rules of your reality are not arbitrary, unyielding structures. Everything in your physical reality you created for a purpose to teach you something important about your potential.

There is nothing in your reality that cannot and has not been broken. Even your scientists are discovering this. Nothing is inviolate. Everything is possible. There is no time. there is no space. There simply is.

If you know how to access and manipulate the light which is what all is made of, you can change this, you can create anything. So what to do now? Be. Simply be.

Look at the richness of all the world around you. Not in judgment – that is separation – but as a vast tapestry to be enfolded within your soul.

Look at all that is around you and pull it into your being. The beauty, the ugliness. The dreadful parts, the glorious parts. They are all part of God. Pull it in. Be not afraid.

The light transmutes all, the light transmutes everything. Darkness cannot stand against it, nothing can stand against a light that simply shines without judgment. Loving. Accepting. Without conditions, without qualification.

Go forth into your world and be that light, that infinite light. Feel the light moving through you, know that everything you see is light. Understand this, feel this, embrace this.

When you do, your lives will change. If you accept this in your heart, your deepest heart, you will see what we see.

If you could but see yourselves as we do, in your richness...you are brilliant, luminous indeed.

Know how grand you are? How much courage it takes to step away from the little, safe rules made by the little, safe minds in your reality? To step into a zero-time space where all is unknown and believe that everything is possible?

To look at all that you have known in all of your lives and know that it has been for the purpose of blindly guiding you to this place. And that all of the structures you have accommodated, that you have built and accepted – in all of your lives – guided by the limitation that your society has accepted. To find the courage to step off your cliff and say, 'I will not be bound by this any longer.' When all that is in your face tells you that beyond the cliff is the shredding darkness of the unknown.

You who came here millennia ago because it seemed intriguing to limit your existence to such an extreme, you who bought all of the pictures and the limitations, and the rules of this playground...and you mastered it. All of the hard lives, all of the hard pain, you mastered it all.

And then you brought yourself to a place where you could look at this and in the face of all the evidence say, 'There has got to be more. I do not allow myself to be limited by the narrow, puny minds of those around me.'

Know how special this is, what you have done?

To have played a game all of your lives, and played it well. All you ever knew – that the game was all there is, there was nothing more, there was nothing beyond that – and you got to this point where you said, 'Enough. There is more.' And you stepped off your cliff, each one of you.

You saw beyond the world you had created with all of its walls, and all of its edges, and all of its victim-hood, and all of its fear, and you said, 'No, I can do better than this.'

So you found a way to begin remembering who you are. Against all evidence, against everything in your face, against people who ridicule those who think such as this. Against all of the yardsticks in your reality that measure the size of everything. You chose to believe something beyond that.

Against all of those old men in golden robes who tell you what to do and how to do it or you will be damned forever. You stepped beyond their fear – and yours – to find the Godself within you.

Everything in your reality was telling you this is all there is. This is all that can be. And you are judged on how well you play this stupid, limited, painful little game. And you said, 'No. I will not believe that.'

That simple action...it was a vast cliff, you will never again have to step off anything harder than that.

You might have started this last step as a game, yourself. 'I will try it, see what happens. I will see if the sky does not open up and swallow me.' But in that possibility, you began to accept that it could be true. And each step, you opened your hearts wider and wider, and then began to feel the reality of what you hoped was true. In that trust, that choice to believe what is in the face of everything you ever knew, that was such an act of personal courage. Such an immense leap of faith.

And you ask why we come here to help you?

Because you are the bravest beings in all of the universe, to have done what you have done.

To have overcome all that you have overcome.

To have handicapped yourselves as much as you have.

And in the face of all of that, to still have accomplished all you have accomplished.

Know what you accomplished?

You have changed the prophecies.

You have done this, through your personal courage. You stepped off your individual cliffs, and chose to believe not that which surrounded you, but you chose to believe that which you felt in your hearts.

So, this is your graduation.

Leave here and take what you have learned, felt, known, experienced, blended; take it outside and with your very presence, use your energy to help others raise their energies, their hearts.

This is your new journey, starting with the new you. This is your destiny. And this is your graduation, each one of you who read this book.

We should have a ceremony should we not?

Put up your left hand up, palm out. Close your eyes and feel the ever-so-slight tingling sensation of my hand meeting yours. You think that a face of God who is not bound by time nor space will not know when you are ready for such a bold, transformative gesture? If you do this, I will be there with you.

I am Eloram, and I am here for you. I will always be here for you...you may call upon me at any time.

Whenever you see something wondrous, call upon me and I will smile along with you.

Whenever you look into another's eyes and see the face of your own God reflected back to you, I will be there, sharing the light.

And when you look around your grand and beautiful earth, and recognize that she is you and you are her and this now is your time to shine and protect and love each other, I will be there, celebrating the recognition.

Dear masters, go with love and light.

Afterword

WHAT IS IT TO BE INSPIRED? In Greek, it means the "breath of the gods."

Where does creative thought come from? Where in heaven's name did this book come from and where do these kinds of insights into our reality and our existence come from?

Probably from everything I've ever read, ever thought, ever imagined. From every conversation I've ever had with people who know more than I do, who are better read than I am. Sometimes these ideas would drift around me like whispers of fog, shape-shifting while I tried to make sense of them one word at a time, crafting what at times felt like necklaces where there was only one perfect illusive bead for each place. Sometimes whole pages would appear almost fully formed as I sat at my computer, like Venus from Botticelli's clamshell.

I don't know. As many writers will tell you, it's a mystery.

When I was a child I had an imaginary friend, a tiger, actually, who regaled me with stories and did battle with playground bullies while I tried to sit as small as I could around the edges. He didn't make me feel particularly brave, but he did make me feel protected. To a young child that's probably enough.

I'm sure that explains it perfectly...

Anyway, I asked Eloram how he would describe how this book was written, and in his inimitable way...for he has become whole and living in my mind and more importantly, in my heart...and this is what he 'said':

So you want to talk about the mechanics of this communication?

One answer is, if we are strong enough to choose lives on your planet, are we not clever enough to encourage thoughts to bloom in the fertile gardens of receptive minds? There is such an intimacy in sharing the consciousness of another through this form of interdimensional connection, in the entwining of our separate harmonics into a greater orchestration of communication.

Imagine the connection, imagine the remarkable storehouse of experience we each access in such a dance. You chose to come here to experience so many great things, so you each are fabulous repositories of awareness, of knowledge and unique perspectives. You are each riches, libraries, abundance, each faces of the infinite God. To be allowed to share such a conjoining of awareness in this kind of communion is an extraordinary experience.

We learn greatly from you. We come here to help you for we love you, but also because it is a joyful experience, to be in the presence of those who chose an existence in which you have handicapped yourselves with so many constraints in your world.

So, this process of interdimensional communication. We must share with you that this one had...has...a great deal of trouble allowing for this. The idea of the process conjured up visions of people seated around a table with the lights dim, calling upon ghosts, listening for things that go bump in the night. Either that or someone with glitter on their eyelids, seated on stage in a vast auditorium talking with 'E.T.'

We are amused by those ideas. There are so many in your reality who truly sense that there are realms of existence beyond the apparent, and they seek to communicate with those realms. However, they are unable to relinquish their own perceptions – which are shaped in limitation by the world they have always known. So they reach out for signs, but they warp them through their own prejudice and impose their own narrow expectations onto what they see.

And though there are many in your reality who would scoff at this remarkable process and would label it metaphysical nonsense, nevertheless, there is physics to metaphysics and there are many in your reality who are close to being able to define and measure this kind of transaction. Those who are exploring quantum physics are already looking at it, they are just unsure how to describe it. Words, a product of your limited minds, are at times unable to fully describe an event without limits. Your mathematics then becomes a much more eloquent language, able to articulate concepts barely grasped by the literate mind.

So, this process...it is a challenge. There is a great disparity of energies between you who've chosen to limit your expression of being with third-dimensional rules within this reality, and those such as myself who exist in higher dimensional states. You operate within a range of frequencies defined by your dimension, we operate within a greatly expanded range that includes much higher frequencies. Plus, each individual consciousness operates with a set of frequencies that define the unique nature of that individual. The challenge is to find one whose frequency is in relative harmony with ours, one who resonates with our essential being.

Understand that the essential being of the person in this reality helps define that part of us which can be expressed. For we search the rich library of that individual for information, concepts, memories, experiences, perceptions, data, feelings...to help us translate what we wish to say in a manner you can understand.

So, what you hear are the cohesive intentions that created my consciousness, creating a 'meta-consciousness' you might say, with the individual consciousness of this person. And this meta-consciousness is what creates communication such as this book.

This is not a particularly uncommon phenomenon in your reality. Most within your dimension, however, have imposed their own pictures and definitions on the process and have labeled it everything from inspiration to prayer to dialogue with one's higher self.

In a way, all are true.

I think the more important question is what does this book say to you? Does it empower you? Does it make you feel the potential to create a happier life?

Simpler still, is the message a good one? And that, dear ones, is your choice.

Michelle Duarte and Eloram,

Oregon 2015

If you want to continue your conversation with Eloram, visit his blog: Eloram.info.

ABOUT THE AUTHOR

Michelle Duarte was a copywriter in advertising for too many years to count. She wound up as an executive creative director/director of creative services for an international ad agency on Madison Avenue. She quit the agency and the career and moved back home to Los Angeles where she decided to start over in her life. She was in L.A. during the big Northridge quake in 1994, which became both a signpost and a push in her journey to create a better and more satisfying future.

What if, she wondered, there could a friendly visitor from the stars who could take the long view and help us on planet earth make sense of such frightening events around us. And that was the start of her new path. She studied meditation, philosophy, psychology, anthropology, alternative spiritual paths, counseling, quantum physics, comparative religion,

New Age mysticism. She even took a two-year accredited course to earn her Masters of Divinity, but balks at the title Reverend "I think that is better earned with a longer history of devotion."

She was both curious and cynical, and decided to rest when she reached hopeful. It felt like a very long way from where she started.

Then she fell in love and decided that all things were possible.

She remarried and now lives with her husband, Dean, and their cat, Miss Scarlett, in Oregon in a small town with no stop lights where they built and operate a small, eco-friendly resort. She misses New York pizza and L.A. chili rellenos. The rest, not so much.

Acknowledgements

This book grew over a 20-year period. I can't even begin to remember all the helpful and generous souls who introduced me to new ideas, new life options. Who applauded my baby steps. Who helped me understand a different way of moving through life. Who read parts of this manuscript and gave me valuable insights and criticisms. Who tackled the whole thing and helped with ideas and flow.

A few, though are indelible: Melissa Halsey, my first real spiritual teacher who pointed a flashlight down a new and unsettling path while I was living in New York. The Phoenix and Bodhi Tree bookstores in Los Angeles where I explored that increasingly disruptive journey. Laura Bajkowski who helped me start the conversations that led to Eloram at the very beginning. She read, listened, discussed and encouraged me in this massive effort. Jim Robinson, an art director partner of mine from my advertising days who read an earlier version of this and said it should be published. What a spur that was. Ana Gordon, who got me to do it now, when it might do some good. And of course, my husband, Dean, who found me, taught me how to love again, showed me what family really means, and helped me talk through all of this. He helped refine the concepts, asked really good questions, talked me down from the ledge a few times, and made all the space I needed to focus on this when the time was right. And, his great eye caught nits and inconsistencies even my obsessive copywriting background missed. Ain't love grand.